The Secret to Everything

The Secret to Everything

Cheryle M. Touchton
Author of Pocket Full of Quarters

Pleasant Word
A Division of WinePress Group

© 2010 by Pocket Full of Change Ministries. All rights reserved.

Pleasant Word (a division of WinePress Publishing, PO Box 428, Enumclaw, WA 98022) functions only as book publisher. As such, the ultimate design, content, editorial accuracy, and views expressed or implied in this work are those of the author.

No part of this publication may be reproduced, stored in a retrieval system, or transmitted in any way by any means—electronic, mechanical, photocopy, recording, or otherwise—without the prior permission of the copyright holder, except as provided by USA copyright law.

Unless otherwise noted, all Scriptures are taken from the *Holy Bible, New International Version®, NIV®*. Copyright © 1973, 1978, 1984 by Biblica, Inc.™ Used by permission of Zondervan. All rights reserved worldwide. WWW.ZONDERVAN.COM

Scripture references marked ASV are taken from the *American Standard Version* of the Holy Bible first published in 1901 by Thomas Nelson and Sons.

Scripture references marked KJV are taken from the *King James Version* of the Bible.

Scripture references marked THE MESSAGE are taken from *The Message Bible* © 1993 by Eugene N. Peterson, NavPress, PO Box 35001, Colorado Springs, CO 80935, 4th printing in USA 1994. Published in association with the literary agency—Alive Comm. PO Box 49068, Colorado Springs, CO 80949. Used by permission.

ISBN 13: 978-1-4141-1381-4
ISBN 10: 1-4141-1381-1
Library of Congress Catalog Card Number: 2009901049

This book is lovingly dedicated to the men in my life. My godly grandfather, Von Vera Mosely, demonstrated what a Christian husband is and made me willing to settle for no less. My heroic daddy, Cecil Milligan, is the kind of father every little girl wants, and because of him, I've found it easy to call God "Father." My uncle, Robert Herrington, also calls me daughter, so I've been twice blessed by godly father figures. My brother, Vaughan Milligan, has stayed my friend and playmate throughout my life. I love my brilliant, interesting, and supportive husband, Bob Touchton (RoBob), more today than the day I married him. The next generation of men, our son, son-in-law, nephews, and grandson are already living up to the standards set by their role models. It is easy to love God and people when the men around me demonstrate that principle daily. I thank God every day for wise women who chose such amazing men as husbands.

Contents

Preparation	xi
Promise	xv
Progression:	
Step 1: Progress to—Mind Matters	1
Step 2: Progress to—Heart Helps	21
Step 3: Progress to—Soul Soothers	45
Step 4: Progress to—Strength Solutions	69
Step 5: Progress to—Neighbor Needs	91
Perseverance: The Next Step	121
Parley	127
Endnotes	137

Other Books by Cheryle M. Touchton

Pocket Full of Quarters—5 Steps to Loving God
Pocket Full of Christmas—Having a Purpose Filled Christmas
A Gospel Conversation Framework—How to Share the Gospel Along Your Paths and In Your Circles

Preparation

"I'M STARTING TO feel my body again," Judy said. "I've just been numb." She'd had two close friends to die in one week. That, combined with a series of annoying medical procedures and intense work pressures, had caused her to shut down mentally, emotionally, spiritually, and physically.

Fortunately, my friend and mentor knew a secret. When things became overwhelming, she retreated, focused her energy on God, and made use of her strong support systems. By doing that, she was able to pass through her difficult season.

When things start falling apart, growing stressful, or getting tense, the temptation is to frantically work on meeting every new challenge. The problem is that when many challenges bombard us at once, we find ourselves spiraling out of control in a frenzy of fruitless frustration. There is a better way.

Are you ready to discover *The Secret to Everything*? It will take hard work, but the ancient secret that has enlightened people for centuries can be yours if you want it. You can learn how to deal with those mental, emotional, spiritual, and physical stressors that drain your energy and try to ruin your life.

The Secret to Everything

This book is for personal study with a spiritual mentor or a small group study. Begin by telling your family you will be spending thirty minutes alone every day for the next five weeks. Find a private place where you can concentrate without interruption. Get a journal. Start or join a small accountability group or ask a trustworthy person to act as your spiritual mentor and confidant. Read the *Promise* and proceed to each *Step*. Spend one week on each *Step*. Answer the questions in the *Parley* and use them for weekly group discussions or time with your mentor.

This book has a five-step progression to the treasure everyone seeks:

- Step 1: Mind Matters
- Step 2: Heart Helps
- Step 3: Soul Soothers
- Step 4: Strength Solutions
- Step 5: Neighbor Needs

Each Step has seven Ps:

- Primary Principle: The overriding spiritual principle behind the step
- Purpose: The purpose for the step
- Promise: The promise of the step
- Process: How to climb the step
- Problems: Typical hurdles and excuses we encounter when climbing the step
- Practical Applications: Stories and examples that demonstrate how the step can apply to your life
- Points to Ponder: Final thoughts about the step

When you finish, you will have just begun your adventure. Read the section entitled *"Perseverance,"* and let your new life unfold—one day at a time.

Preparation

Below are daily and weekly suggestions for the next five weeks. If you embrace this secret weapon against every evil, disappointment, and frustration, you will soar as if you are riding on the wings of eagles.

Daily Suggestions

Meditation (3–5 Minutes)

Meditate on the Greatest Commandment (Luke 10:27) and related scriptures.

Prayer (3–5 Minutes)

- Ask God to give you knowledge of His will for you and the power to carry it out.
- Pray and journal the five Ps.
  - Plan—Ask God for wisdom and list your plans for the day.
  - Praise—List your blessings and joys.
  - Pain—Tell God your problems, what hurts, and your concerns.
  - Petition—Ask God for the desires of your heart.
  - Profession—Confess your mistakes, unholy desires, and wayward thoughts from the day before, and make your commitments for the new day.

Bible Study: (10–15 Minutes)

- Steps: There are five of them, so study one per week.
- Ps: Each step has seven Ps.
  - Read and absorb one to two Ps per day.
  - Look up the Scripture references and study the context of the scriptures.
  - Memorize the scriptures marked for memory.

Application (5–10 Minutes)

The most important part of any book is personal application. Personal application can include personal responsibility, confession, change, and action. Spend a few minutes each day journaling what you discover and answering the questions in the *Parley* related to the point you are studying. Take action immediately.

Weekly Suggestions

The section labeled *Parley* contains directions and questions for use with a small accountability group or a personal mentor. Plan a time each week to discuss these questions and make commitments.

Promise

> No eye has seen, no ear has heard, no mind has conceived what God has prepared for those who love him.
>
> —1 Corinthians 2:9

AS I SAT in the Intensive Care waiting room, I didn't think I could stand it. Our family was still recovering from the brutal murder of my husband's great-aunt Jamie, and now my beloved grandfather was in the ICU with a severely damaged heart. As I stared at my grandmother, who was sitting across from me, I wondered if she understood how seriously ill her husband was.

My grandparents had the kind of marriage everyone wanted. They still held hands when they walked. They cuddled when they sat. For sixty years they'd been together almost continually, and before this heart attack, I'd seen little sign of aging. Throughout their lives, they ran businesses together, raised four daughters, and directed music for churches. I was terrified that they were about to be separated.

The ICU only allowed visitors every two hours. The time in between stretched like an eternity, leaving too much time to think. I examined my own life. I was twenty-seven, and so far, I

The Secret to Everything

felt like I had wasted it. I was a Christian, but for some reason, it wasn't enough to satisfy the emptiness in my soul. Things were tense with my own husband. Until just a year before, I'd been bedridden with obesity-related health problems, and everyone had taken care of me. On January 19, 1979, I cried out to God and asked for the sin of gluttony to be removed. I felt God gently promising that if I ate healthy foods in moderate quantities and avoided all foods that had become false gods, He would remove my desire to kill myself with food. I'd spent the last year working on my physical health and was already reaping the rewards.

When it was finally time to visit, I tiptoed into the sterile hospital room. I took a deep breath and felt dizzy from the strong smell of medicine and sickness. I looked at the wires attached to my grandfather and found the hum of the monitors comforting. He looked at me and smiled warmly, "Gal, you've got your school girl figure back." Those were to be the last words he ever spoke to me.

I did indeed look and feel better physically but wondered why I was still so miserable. What was missing? I worried about everything. My husband was often away from home on business, and I resented him because of it. I wanted to do more than I was doing, but fear kept me from trying new things. I called myself a "stay at home mom," but I was really a couch potato, spending my days watching soap operas. I believed the promise that I could do all things through Christ who strengthened me, but for some reason, I just couldn't seem to apply that to my life.

That is the beginning of my story and what motivated me to seek a change. I'll bet you have a story of your own. What if there were an ancient, secret formula—one that was centuries old? Assume for a moment that this formula contained the secret to finding everything we seek for a fulfilled life. While each generation had passed this formula to the next, not all generations had recognized its value or applied its worth. Suppose it was your turn to have this mysterious formula and your research

Promise

indicated those generations that embraced this secret formula soared as if on "eagle's wings" and the generations who ignored it crashed and burned into the ground. What would you do?

You might write a book called *The Secret to Everything*. The secret formula I'm talking about is called the *Sh'ma* (pronounced *Shuh mah*), which is a Hebrew word that means "to hear." The *Sh'ma* is actually the first two words of a section of the Torah and considered by many to be the most important prayer of the Jewish faith. We see it multiple places throughout the Old and New Testaments, and Jesus told us it was the *most* important commandment. What part of *most* do we not understand? The *Sh'ma,* or the Greatest Commandment as the New Testament calls it, is the ancient secret to everything.

It is:

- The secret formula for balance, success, and well-being.
- The secret weapon against every evil, disappointment, and frustration.
- The secret sauce that spices up our lives.

> **The Secret to Everything: The *Sh'ma***
>
> **(New Testament Name:
> The Greatest Commandment)**
>
> *Love the Lord your God with all your heart and with all your soul and with all your strength and with all your mind and love your neighbor as yourself.* (Luke 10:27)

The Secret to Everything

The secret is to love God with all you think, feel, and do. The rest of this book is going to show you how to do that. You can't imagine what God has planned for you once you decide to do nothing but love Him more. The answer to *everything* in life is to stop working on *every* problem, issue, challenge, annoyance, disappointment, hurdle, or frustration and start using all your energy to love God more. If you love God with your *entire* mind, heart, soul, and strength, you will automatically love your neighbors as yourself. When you fully love God and your neighbors, your desires and dreams will have metamorphosed into full alignment with God's will for your life. You will have that perfect, promised peace that is beyond any earthly explanation. You will have discovered the secret to everything.

Progression

Step 1
Progress to— Mind Matters

And thou shalt love the Lord thy God with all thy mind.

—Mark 12:30 (KJV)

MIND

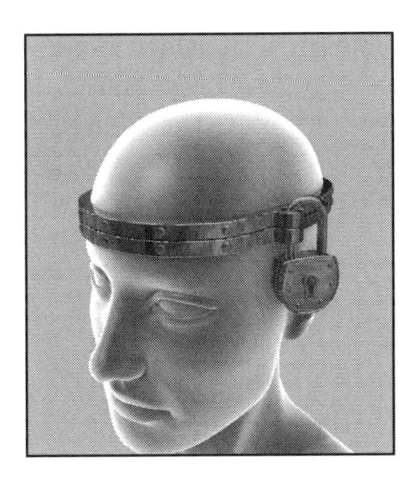

MY CHURCH KNEW our family was going through a difficult time. While I was waiting for news on my grandfather, one of our pastors visited the ICU and asked what he could do.

The Secret to Everything

"We need quarters," I'd said. This was before cell phones, and everything took quarters. There was a phone booth right outside the ICU waiting room, and we needed quarters to call and give medical updates to concerned family and friends. When we grew hungry or thirsty in the middle of the night, we needed quarters for vending machines.

The next time this pastor came, he brought a role of quarters. Up until that point, I'd sat isolated in the corner of the hospital waiting room. My only dialogue with the families of other patients had revolved around asking others if they had quarters. For some reason, when my pastor brought that roll of quarters, I opened it and put the quarters on the table. When people needed quarters, they took them. When they had extra quarters, they put them in the pile. For the rest of the stay, we all had enough quarters.

Sharing those quarters caused me to start talking with the people around me. We shared our medical news and our concerns. Mary, a young woman about my age, and I grew friendly. Mary's daddy was in the ICU, and she was terrified just like I was. We were both Christians and wondered where the promised peace that passes all understanding was hiding.

I thought about my grandparents' lives. Their lives hadn't been easy and yet they were happy. Two of their daughters suffered from chronic mental illness. I can remember my grandmother saying, "Von and I would sit at the piano singing hymns, crying, and praying for our girls." How could they be happy in the middle of so much sorrow? I knew the answer lay in the fact that they aligned their mind with the mind of Christ. I wondered how they did that.

I knew the Bible promised we could have the mind of Christ. That process starts with inviting Jesus into our lives. As a young child, I'd believed in Jesus, confessed my sin, and asked Him to become a part of my life. I knew I was a Christian and that if I died, I'd go to heaven. However, I was a long way from having the mind of Christ.

Progress to—Mind Matters

> **The secret to making good decisions is to love God with your entire mind.**

More than once in my life, I've taken an ill-advised action and later asked myself the question, *What was I thinking?* The truthful answer is that while I was doing a lot of obsessing about what I wanted or needed, I was doing little thinking about loving God with my entire mind. Ever since I finally had that simple concept drilled into my seemingly concrete head—the notion that every decision and thought should be about loving God with my mind—my life has gone much better. I discovered that *the secret to making good decisions is to love God with my entire mind.*

Step 1 unlocks our minds, freeing them from the thoughts that imprison our lives. The premise of this step is that almost everyone who finds himself or herself depressed, obsessed, overwhelmed, worried, or disappointed will find immediate relief if he or she focuses all of that energy on loving God with his or her entire mind. The spiritual principle of Step 1 is that we can have the mind of Christ. In order to have that mind, we must first become His disciples and study God's Word, the Bible. Once we have the mind of Christ, we gain true knowledge, knowledge of Christ and of what is best for us. The secret to this step is that having the mind of Christ unlocks every other secret.

Primary Principle:
You Can Have the Mind of Christ

Memory Verse:

But we have the mind of Christ.

—1 Corinthians 2:16

The Secret to Everything

I was angry about Bob's great aunt Jamie being murdered. A traveling serial killer had broken into her home and killed her. I grieved and lived in terror for weeks that the same thing would happen to me. In one of my study groups, I asked, "How could God have let this happen? I'm so mad. Aunt Jamie was a sweet, elderly Christian woman. The man that did this should be drawn and quartered."

A woman about five feet tall stood up, pointed her finger at me, and shouted, "Honey, your aunt is in heaven. Your job is to love and forgive the man who did this. That is what Jesus did. He died for murderers too. God will deal with that man the way He sees fit."

I was shocked. *How could she be so insensitive to my pain?* Then, God answered. The mind of Christ offered grace to sinners, and I could have that mind. The mind of Christ forgave those who murdered Him, before they repented. When I let the grace offered by the mind of Christ wash over me, I was able to forgive a murderer who tore my family apart. When I forgave him, I felt the first peace I'd felt in weeks.

If you invite Jesus to participate in your life journey, become His disciple, and study the Word of God, over time, you can have the mind of Christ! Think about that for a moment. How could one possibly suffer from low self-esteem, obsession, or depression with the mind of Christ? The mind of Christ is perfection. The secret to having His mind is to study and apply the Bible. How could you fail to succeed with the mind of Christ? The Bible says you can do all things through Christ (Phil. 4:13). As you study the rest of this step, let this overriding spiritual principle guide you. You *can* have the mind of Christ.

Purpose: Discipleship

The purpose of loving God with your mind is to become a disciple of Jesus. Becoming a disciple is more than just becoming

Progress to—Mind Matters

a Christian. Think back to the original twelve disciples. They were Jewish men taught to love God. A brilliant teacher and impressive Rabbi walked up and invited them to follow. We do not know much about how those young men, probably teenagers most of them,[1] made the intellectual decision to follow Jesus, but one has to wonder if their mothers shouted, *"Are you crazy?"* Imagine leaving jobs and loved ones to follow someone many actually considered crazy. The disciples certainly did not have all the answers and could not have dreamed what would be in front of them. Their journeys toward love started with becoming a disciple of Jesus. Being His disciple became their purpose in life, their reason for living, and eventually their reason for dying.

I accepted Christ as my personal Savior at age eight, but as you have heard, I did not understand what it meant to become His disciple until years later. Now, my Shetland Sheepdog, Belle, and I travel the streets of America several months a year as missionaries. I get up in the morning and ask God where to go. I get in my tiny camper van, Halleluiah, and stop anywhere I see people. God prepares the hearts of the people He sends my way. I am thrilled when I get to be with someone who prays to receive Jesus for the first time, but I know that joyous event is just the beginning of a long journey.

One overwhelming observation I have made as I travel is how many troubled Christians there are. Many Christians are still hopelessly battling and losing their own personal wars to control their earthly circumstances. When they fail, they blame themselves or others and become as bitter as the rind of a lemon.

What if after you accepted Jesus as your personal Savior you truly stopped whining, studied your Bible, bore your crosses, and ran after Jesus? To "bear a cross" means to accept unpleasant circumstances that you cannot change. What if Christians accepted the heavy burden of earthly circumstances and turned their minds towards learning everything there was to learn from Jesus? I know what would happen; the same thing that happened to the disciples. Crosses would feel weightless. The Bible says it and I've personally experienced it. Jesus' yoke is easy and the burden of those crosses becomes light. The circumstances might or might not improve, but Christians would find rest for their souls.

> **Keys to Discipleship**
>
> 1. Say "Yes" to Salvation.
> 2. Bear Your Crosses.
> 3. Learn From the Word of God.

Say "Yes" to Salvation

> For God so loved the world, that he gave his only begotten Son, that whosoever believeth in him should not perish, but have everlasting life.
>
> —John 3:16 (KJV)

Salvation is the secret to eternal life with God and the first key to discipleship. God loved you so much that He sent His Son to earth to be your Savior and Teacher. Jesus was born to a virgin, died on a cross, and rose from the dead. He was fully man and fully God. When you accept the facts of His birth, death, and resurrection; confess your need for Him and your sins to Him; and invite Him to be your Savior and the Shepherd of your soul, God saves you for all eternity.

Bear Your Crosses

> Whosoever doth not bear his cross, and come after me, cannot be my disciple.
>
> —Luke 14:27 (KJV)

Progress to—Mind Matters

"I want to come home," I wailed over the phone. I was 2,000 miles away, broken down beside the road, wet, and cold.

"I know, Baby," Bob said, already looking for someone to repair Halleluiah. We both knew I wouldn't come home. What I would do was get Halleluiah fixed and watch for the special evangelical assignment that came out of the latest adventure.

Bob and I have a call to the streets of America. Bob's call is to help support my journeys, navigate, pray for me, edit my writing, and help get me out of jams. His crosses are to feel helpless when he can't help me and do without his wife for months at a time. I'm a missionary. My call is to travel three to four months per year, evangelizing, exhorting, exorcising, educating, encouraging, and easing burdens. My crosses are to get lost, break down, be lonely, and stay tired. This call is a joyous one, but it does come with crosses to bear.

Bearing your crosses is the second key to discipleship and forms the bridge between your salvation and ability to learn. The term comes from Jesus willingly dying on the cross. He did not let the fear of horrendous pain that would lead to a slow, agonizing death keep Him from being obedient. To bear your crosses means you accept your earthly circumstances and your calling from God, and you allow God to use them and you.

I meet people who remind me of a wild, bucking bronco as they desperately try to toss the weight of their crosses from their backs. Those crosses cling to their backs, and the effort of all that jumping, bending, and tossing wears out even the sturdiest of wild horses.

When you accept the burdens and follow Christ, bent back and all, you begin to find peace. Wonder of wonders, instead of the crosses distracting you, they strengthen you.

The Secret to Everything

Learn

> Take my yoke upon you, and learn from me; for I am meek and lowly in heart: and ye shall find rest unto your souls. For my yoke is easy, and my burden is light.
>
> —Matthew 11:29–30 (KJV)

The final key to discipleship and the secret to loving God with all your mind is to take His yoke and learn. You learn by listening to God, reading your Bible, sitting in Bible studies, going to church, accepting your responsibilities, and carrying your crosses. As your mind merges with the mind of Christ, those burdens grow light and chains fall away. You will have unlocked your mind.

Promise: Knowledge

Memory Verse:

> For this very reason, make every effort to add to your faith goodness; and to goodness, knowledge.
>
> —2 Peter 1:5

Faith → Goodness → Knowledge

For most of my life, I've been a student of the Bible. I read it, even when I couldn't seem to apply much of it to my life. Step 1 is about gaining knowledge, but that is only the beginning. When my heart, soul, and strength finally caught up with my mind, my life started working.

The promise of loving God with your mind is knowledge. The Bible says *to study and show yourself approved unto God* (2 Timothy 2:15). When you decide to follow Jesus and stop complaining, fretting, debating, or rationalizing, there is room in your head for knowledge. The energy spent on these intellectual struggles and debates transforms into a desire to know how to improve. After all, if you are not going to improve your self-esteem by rationalizing, you need to learn how to handle those unruly thoughts playing tug-of war in your head. The journey starts with faith. Faith begins when you accept Jesus as your Savior. Goodness follows faith as you take up your cross (which means to stop whining, fretting, debating, or rationalizing) and follow Jesus' example.

Goodness then leads to knowledge as you study God's Word, the Bible, and learn. By reading the Bible, you learn simple secrets like:

- Think about what is lovely (Philippians 4:8).
- Stop debating and arguing (Job 15:2–5).
- Study (2 Timothy 2:15).
- Ignore distractions (Proverbs 4:25 The Message).

Gaining knowledge begins with the study of the Bible, but it does not stop there. When you have the mind of Christ, you discover what role Christ wants you to fulfill in the world. Accepting your assignments and fulfilling them to Christ's standards may take additional study.

For example, at one time, Christ called me to run a business. One of the ways I gained knowledge about how to run a business was to get a Masters of Business Administration. No one would want to use a doctor, electrician, or trash collector who did not have the appropriate knowledge to practice his or her trade. When God calls us to fulfill an earthly role, He expects and will make a way for us to get the appropriate education.

Life also offers opportunities for gaining knowledge. I was a better parent with my third child than with my first because I'd learned more. Part of our responsibility as we travel our journey through life is to learn from our circumstances and apply that knowledge to our futures. The Bible tells us to be *workmen that*

The Secret to Everything

need never be ashamed (2 Timothy 2:15) and to *work as if all work is for God* (Colossians 3:23).

Process

> You were taught, with regard to your former way of life, to put off your old self, which is being corrupted by its deceitful desires; to be made new in the attitude of your minds; and to put on the new self, created to be like God in true righteousness and holiness.
>
> —Ephesians 4:22–24

So, how do you change your attitudes? How do you begin loving God with your entire mind? The answer is simple. Ephesians 4:22–24 clearly spells it out.

Putting On New Attitudes

1. **Put off your old self.**
2. **Let God make you new in the attitude of your mind.**
3. **Put on your new self.**

First, you put off your nasty old self, the one who worries, whines, blames, and/or pouts. You simply stomp your feet at Satan and say, "No more!"

Second, you let Jesus make you new in the attitude of your mind. You confess sin and ask Him to forgive you. You beg Him to teach you and give you His mind.

Third, you study your Bible, and through the power of the Holy Spirit, you put on your brand new shiny self, and become someone who:

Progress to—Mind Matters

- Disciplines your thoughts.
- Thinks about what is lovely.
- Studies everything you need to know, spiritually and personally, so you are approved by God.
- Has the wondrous, intelligent, creative, mind-blowing mind of Christ.

PROBLEMS: YES, BUT…

At this point you may be arguing, "Yes, but I already know everything you've written. *Why* am I not practicing it?" If you are a mature Christian who regularly studies the Bible, often you know what to do. However, actually doing it is another matter entirely.

Jesus said, "…the spirit is willing, but the body is weak" (Matthew 26:41). The apostle Paul admitted he found himself doing what he didn't want to do (Romans 7:15). If you feel the same way, you are in good company; but that is no excuse for inaction. One clue that you might be about to give into weak flesh is hearing yourself say the perilous words, "Yes, but." Those two tiny words negate every good thing you have thought, read, or heard. They become the excuse for why godly wisdom does not apply to you and allow you to begin slipping and sliding down the slimy slope of disobedience, disappointment, and despair. This section includes some of the more common "Yes, buts" that relate to each step.

Yes, But Unruly Thoughts Continue to Taunt Me

Unruly thoughts can ruin your days and life. When one of my girlfriends allows circumstances to overwhelm and confuse her, she says, "My mind is spaghetti." If you allow them, unruly thoughts will taunt and terrorize you, turning your mind into slippery, dripping spaghetti that refuses to wind around a fork and ends up dripping greasy stains onto your clothes. The Bible is clear about how to handle those bossy nuisances:

- Take your thoughts captive: "We demolish arguments and every pretension that sets itself up against the knowledge of God, and we take captive every thought to make it obedient to Christ" (2 Corinthians 10:5–6).

- Whatever is lovely, think on these things: "Finally, brethren, whatsoever things are true, whatsoever things are honest, whatsoever things are just, whatsoever things are pure, whatsoever things are lovely, whatsoever things are of good report; if there be any virtue, and if there be any praise, think on these things" (Philippians 4:8 KJV).

Yes, But I Like Debating

> If you were truly wise, would you sound so much like a windbag, belching hot air? Would you talk nonsense in the middle of a serious argument, babbling baloney? Look at you! You trivialize religion, turn spiritual conversation into empty gossip. It's your sin that taught you to talk this way.
>
> —Job 15:2–5 (The Message)

Debating is a favorite American pastime. No matter how good you are at debating, there will always be someone better. Debates may start out fun, but they usually turn sour. They have no winners. Yes, you may score points and briefly get ahead, but a worthy opponent will gather more information and strike when you are most vulnerable. When it comes to eternal, spiritual matters, debating is wrong. So:

- Stop belching hot air.
- Stop turning spiritual conversation into empty gossip.

- Memorize the phrase: "You may be right." ("Be completely humble and gentle…" [Ephesians 4:2]).
- State your position once and leave it alone.

Yes, But I'm Disappointed With My Educational Achievements

Study to show thyself approved unto God.

—2 Timothy 2:15 (KJV)

If you hear yourself apologizing for your lack of education, it may be because you need more education to fulfill God's call on your life.

- It is never too late to be the person God wants you to be today.
- Ask God what He wants you to do.
- Do what you have been longing to do, as long as it is not contrary to Scripture.
- Be faithful to study—after all, you have the mind of Christ.

Yes, But I'm Not Smart Enough

Were you not listening? You can have the mind of Christ! If that is not smart enough for you, you have a bigger problem than we can talk about in this point. Here's what I suggest:

- Rebuke negative thoughts about yourself.
- Remind yourself that you can have the mind of Christ!

Practical Applications

So how might all of this apply to your daily life? Let me offer some practical applications from my life and the lives of people

The Secret to Everything

I have met on the streets of America. Perhaps you can think of a few of your own and write them in a journal.

Family Wars

Does your family play the action-packed, high-energy game of *Family Wars*? You know the game. It starts with pontificating about religion, politics, or the family past. Everyone starts talking at once, and the volume rises. You know you are about to score a point when the children run and hide. Mix a little alcohol in, and it can get downright dangerous.

Gender bashing is a popular round in *Family Wars*. Men are famous for their "wife jokes," and women love to get together and entertain each other with the Neanderthal antics of their hapless husbands. Teenage behavior offers the perfect temptation for parents to gossip about their children by telling stories that are perhaps amusing to the adults but humiliating to the objects of the stories. Personally, I wish someone had warned me when I had small children that *everything* I said and did would be fair game for public dinnertime conversation for the *rest* of my life.

The game of *Family Wars* begins in the mind. The problem with *Family Wars* is that the seemingly harmless fun hurls our minds down the slippery slope of negativity. Once we start playing this exciting game of *Family Wars*, it is hard to stop. If you are addicted to *Family Wars*, take heart; the mind of Christ offers grace. We can do all things through Christ. We can stop focusing on what is wrong with our poor relatives and start thinking about all the lovely things they do and say… *even if the list is short*. Life might not be as exciting, but when you see your relatives through the grace-giving mind of Christ, you will like them much better.

Curiosity Usually Doesn't Kill Cats

People use the popular expression "curiosity killed the cat" to warn children venturing into dangerous territory. The fact is, curiosity

Progress to—Mind Matters

is a good thing and does not usually kill cats. Curiosity is at the heart of scientific progress and our spiritual growth and should never be discouraged in children.

During my missionary journeys, I've visited every state in the nation. I've sat on beach blankets with young mothers and their children, watching the mothers struggle to put sunscreen on their wriggling imps. I've hiked National Parks alongside young families doing their best to keep their precious darlings from leaping off the side of a cliff. I've helped a father disentangle his curious two-year old from a briar patch.

Sometimes I am appalled by what I hear parents say to their children. Knowing that *what* we say is a result of what we *think*, I have to wonder what is going on in their minds about their children. I shudder when I hear parents laughing and calling their children self-esteem-destroying words like "nosey," "bad," "fat," "chubby," or "bossy." *Why would they spend even a moment thinking those thoughts about the precious little ones they love so much?* I was hurt by the name calling of other children when I was a child, and when I see parents taunting their own children, I remember the pain of humiliating words.

I watched a young father holding his curious daughter. This bright-eyed, three-month-old wonder was watching everything. Her tiny eyes darted back and forth as she watched in awe.

"Look at her," I trilled. "She's amazing. She is watching everything."

"Yes," the father said. "She's nosey all right."

I wondered what would make him think such a thing. *Could a baby even be nosey?* "Don't say that," I bluntly snapped before I could stop myself. "Your beautiful infant isn't nosey. She is delightfully curious." I regretted not taking the time to pray before I spoke and was fortunate this father didn't turn his negative vocabulary on me.

Name-calling, even in jest, does damage. Just ask my girlfriend Janice Sullivan. She is an intelligent, curious bright light, who has spent her life seeking knowledge. She is an avid reader and loves words so much that she carries a dictionary in her purse. She does me the honor of reading my words and giving me honest feedback. She craves knowledge. When she was a child, her family saw that impressive curiosity drive but chose to tease her about it by calling her the nasty name, "nosey." It took her years to appreciate her natural curiosity that we all enjoy so much today.

Words matter, especially words spoken to children. Thoughts precede words. To control words, we must discipline our thoughts. Negative words to children are not a joke. They will believe what you tell them. Curiosity doesn't usually kill cats, but words may kill curious minds.

With Whom Are You Arguing?

"A degree doesn't matter," one of my peers announced in a staff meeting. "It means nothing." We'd been reviewing technical resumes and were discussing the potential candidates for a job opening. In the course of the year I'd worked with this man, I'd heard him make that statement several times. He was an excellent employee, but I knew he'd never finished college. I wondered with whom he was arguing and suspected it was himself.

I met a young Vietnamese woman who professed her spiritual journey from Buddhism to Christianity. The testimony brought tears to my eyes as she talked about her personal walk with Jesus and how she had to fight her parents when she converted. Then, she ended by saying, "My priest keeps talking about reading the Bible. I don't need to read the Bible. It's too hard. I couldn't understand it anyway. Going to church is enough." Bless her heart. She was arguing with her priest, and he was not even there. I knew better than to argue or tell her what to do. She would have just argued back. Instead, I smiled and gave her my testimony about how much I love reading the words of God.

Progress to—Mind Matters

If you feel defensive or insecure about any educational shortfall, academically, theologically, or spiritually, the mind of Christ is probably trying to tell you something. A college degree is simply a tool for learning and is certainly not necessary for everyone. What is necessary is being properly educated for discipleship. We love God with our entire minds by educating ourselves to be the best at whatever life He calls us to live, professionally and personally.

True Confessions from the Happily Married

Do not attempt to write a book with the bold title *The Secret to Everything*, unless you expect God to teach you a thing or two. The lessons only get harder if you try to write about having the mind of Christ. Some lessons are easy and some painfully sad. I went away to Phoenix, Arizona, to spend a month alone to write this book, and God began sending lessons even as I prepared to travel to Phoenix.

The plan was for Bob and me to vacation in our camper van, Halleluiah, from our Jacksonville Beach home to our Phoenix home. After a few days in Phoenix, Bob would fly back to Jacksonville Beach. At the end of the month, he planned to return to Phoenix and camp with me back to Jacksonville Beach. My Sheltie, loyal, lovable Belle, always travels with me when I drive. She sits under my feet when I write, cuddles with me when I'm lonely, and barks if I get distracted. The lessons began when Bob wanted to vacation with his cat, Rascal.

"I don't want the cat," I said.

"Rascal will be traumatized if I board him that long. He can stay with you and travel back with us."

"Bob," I argued, "Rascal is a distraction. The camper is small, and cat litter smells. He'll bug me when I'm writing."

"I want to take the cat," Bob argued.

Sighing, I reluctantly agreed.

The Secret to Everything

The next lesson was about television. Our Phoenix home was for sale, and we'd turned off all unnecessary services. I looked forward to a month without the temptation of my favorite shows. When we arrived in Phoenix, Bob started hooking up the television.

"Bob," I said, "I don't want television."

"You say that now, but after a week of the silence, you'll want it," he said, busily hooking wires together. It isn't easy to temporarily turn on the cable feed to a television. It took days and involved cable companies, money, newly-purchased equipment, and two trips to a store. By the time my technical wizard husband had finished, not only did I have television, but also he had our digital video recorder working and had programmed it to record my shows.

Through it all, I kept saying, "But I don't want television."

Bob soon left, and I started writing. Rascal was the rascal he always is. When I cooked, he stole my food. He howled at night if I closed him out and jumped on my head while I was sleeping if I let him in. Dishes crashed down from counters and startled me awake at night. Rascal chewed cords, chairs, cell phone ear buds, flowers, and books. He hid things from me and darted into the desert when I let Belle outside. Perfect Belle abandoned me to continuously tussle noisily with the cat, and I realized I was jealous of a cat. I had to feed and water Rascal and change disgusting cat litter. I tried practicing having lovely thoughts about Rascal, and while he is cute, he is still a distracting rascal.

I must be weak about television. I tried to write about self-discipline while thoughts of television shows taunted me. I rationalized that everyone needed a break and wasted hours of writing time. Plots from the shows *House* and *Law and Order* tried to snake their way into this book. I knew I was in trouble when I started recording reruns.

While I was writing about having the mind of Christ, a painful realization struck me. God had given me the mind of Christ when

Progress to—Mind Matters

He prompted me to leave Rascal home and not have the television hooked up. The mind of Christ knew I needed complete focus. Bob, wanting what was best for the cat and me, did not believe what I said about distractions. I called Bob and said the words every husband dreads, "Honey, we need to talk."

As I explained what I'd discovered, Bob recognized the truth and was horrified. We realized that if one of us had the mind of Christ and the other ignored it or talked his or her partner into not listening, we were actually defying Christ together. Bob hadn't believed that the cat and the television would distract me and thought he knew best. I let it happen.

It turns out that the cat and television were silly, inconsequential examples of a bigger marital problem. Throughout the month, God sent many examples of how Bob and I had defied Christ that same way. God even brought some forgotten examples to mind in my dreams. Many memories were serious, and the experiences had disastrous, painful consequences.

Bob and I wanted to weep as we remembered an unsafe babysitter we left our young children with many years before. I was uncomfortable, but Bob thought I needed an evening out. This babysitter was convenient, but I was nervous leaving the children with him. Bob thought I was being overprotective, and since I too wanted to go out, we both ignored my God-given motherly instincts. The result was what I had feared and put our children in serious danger. It is only by the grace of God that something more serious didn't happen.

We walked back through our years of running a business together. I had the business background, and Bob was the technologist. While running our company, I woke up every morning and spent time in prayer, meditation, and Bible Study. Daily, I asked for God's wisdom in regards to our business decisions. God's wisdom combined with my business expertise made my financial and business predictions uncannily accurate, but Bob and I repeatedly ignored those God-given business instincts in favor of

The Secret to Everything

taking an action that was easier and/or more exciting. The result was that we ended up selling a business we loved owning.

Those lessons hurt as we walked back through painful times in our marriage and gained understanding about the causes. It was intimate as we shared our pain without getting too terribly defensive. We knew God was doing a mighty work that would make a good marriage better.

Bob and I are in love, and we have each other's best interests at heart. I usually write wonderful things about our marriage but felt led to share this honest true confession. I write this with Bob's permission and agreement. Bob and I usually learn our spiritual lessons well, and this is one we will not forget. In the future, we plan to stop trying to figure out what is best for the other person and to believe what he or she says. Responsibility accompanies seeking the mind of Christ as a couple. The responsibility is to respect and believe what your partner is telling you and honor it.

Points to Ponder

If you learned just one thing from this chapter, I pray it was the realization of what it could mean for you to have the mind of Christ. All things would be possible. With the mind of Christ, everything that tortures your overworked mind and keeps you awake at night would lift. You would have that wonderful feeling we call "hope." Gone would be your sense of intellectual inadequacy, because you would have the knowledge you need to deal with your life. As God's answers come to you one by one, some of which you may like and others that you may not, you have the knowledge that every answer was for your good. Knowing you can have the mind of Christ is the secret to loving God with your entire mind. The secret to unlocking your mind is to focus your thoughts on what is lovely and rebuke all other thoughts.

Step 2
Progress to—Heart Helps

And thou shalt love the Lord thy God with all thy heart.

—Mark 12:30

MIND → HEART

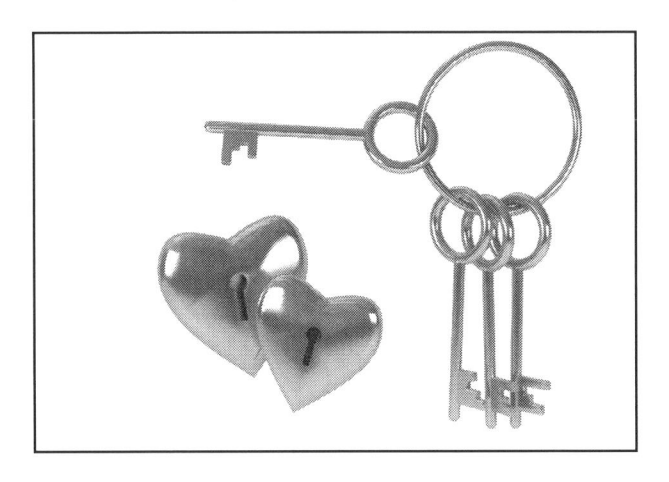

IT WAS THE middle of the night in the ICU waiting room. My grandmother hadn't gone home since my grandfather's heart attack. Mama and Aunt Ka Ka had been taking turns staying with her and were exhausted. On this night, I insisted that I could take a turn. They were surprised and unsure if I could handle things, but after some encouragement, they left me and went home.

There were only two people in the ICU—my grandfather and the father of my new friend Mary. Mary and I waited in the ICU waiting room, she with her mother and I with my grandmother. We tried to sleep, but the chairs were uncomfortable. We finally gave up and just talked. All of a sudden, alarms started blaring. We heard a code called from the ICU, and Mary and I looked at each other worriedly. Something terrible was happening with either my grandfather or her father. The older women were deep in thought and had missed the commotion. Mary and I stepped outside into the hall.

We went to the door of the ICU. People rushed in and out, and we tried to peek inside. A nurse bumped into us and said firmly, "Get out of the way!"

Since we didn't want to alarm the older women by going back into the waiting room, we stepped inside of the phone booth, where we had used so many of those quarters. We were close, closer then I was comfortable standing to someone whom I barely knew. We fidgeted self-consciously, until one of us said, "Let's pray."

We collapsed into one another's arms and started praying. "Please, God," we begged through our tears, "help us." We prayed for our loved one in the ICU, for the women in the waiting room, and for our strength.

Instantly, I felt a power and strength flow through me that I had never felt before. It was as if my head knowledge about the power of Jesus aligned with my heart and my feelings. I stood up straight and knew I could face whatever happened next. I walked out of that phone booth feeling both lighter and stronger than I'd ever felt before. When the nurse walked toward me to say that my grandfather had gone home to be with God, it broke my heart, but I knew I could do all things through Christ who strengthened me.

I went back to the waiting room and gave my grandmother the worst news of her life. I held her, and we rocked and sobbed. I called her doctor, and he ordered her some medicine. I called my mama and Aunt Ka Ka, and God gave me the words to say. This brokenhearted woman, who had so recently been taken care of by everyone, was planning a funeral, taking care of details, and meeting the needs of the brokenhearted around her.

> **Applying the *Sh'ma* to emotion is the secret to emotional balance and maturity.**

Have you ever said the words, "My heart aches?" Unless you were actually having a heart attack, you probably meant that you were sad, distraught, or troubled. Your actual pain was nowhere near the proximity of your thumping heart. Feelings of fear cause your heart to race. Anxiety raises blood pressure and can cause heart attacks. But if you accuse someone of being heartless, you probably mean that person doesn't care about others. "Heart" is a word commonly used to describe emotion. Emotions whirl and twirl out of control, often making you feel like a ping-pong ball in the game of life.

Applying the *Sh'ma* to emotion is the secret to emotional balance and maturity. In Step 1, we unlocked our minds by focusing our thoughts on what is lovely. In Step 2, we unlock our hearts by focusing our affections on loving God.

Let us look at the emotional journey of the young, enthusiastic disciples. As they began spending time with Jesus and growing to love Him more, their emotions raged, occasionally out of control. They fought over who would be first in Jesus' kingdom. They grew angry when people tried to interrupt Jesus.

The Secret to Everything

They trembled in fear when a storm threatened to swamp their boat. They angrily accused Jesus of not caring because He slept as lightening crackled and popped around them and waves surged over the bow of the boat. In a fit of rage, Peter cut off the ear of a soldier who was trying to hurt Jesus. While these emotional mood swings clearly indicated how the disciples' hearts felt about Jesus, Jesus rebuked them and encouraged the disciples to relax and calm down. Over time, these young men learned to control their tumultuous emotions and eventually turned those strong feelings into powerful tools for God.

ARE EMOTIONS RUNNING YOUR LIFE?

The spiritual principle of this step is that God takes great delight in us. Loving God with our hearts is a step in our journeys towards being delighted with God. We often stumble at this step when circumstances bring up more emotions than we want to feel. Some let emotions spin out of control and into anger or violence. Others lock up emotionally and refuse to feel, thus freezing themselves spiritually. Many wallow in the "feel good" emotion of religion, refusing to move any deeper, and when disappointment or tragedy breaks their hearts, they fall away from church and/or God. Some refuse to let God heal their broken hearts. It is hard to love fully with a broken, bruised, or frozen heart.

The purpose of loving God with our hearts is fellowship—with God and people. Godly understanding comes from fellowship. The secret to emotional maturity is to fellowship with Jesus and people. Only through this fellowship can we understand our feelings, take the mature and godly actions these feelings warrant, and then, let them pass. When we focus all of our energy on loving God with our entire hearts, we can grow to where painful and useless hurts, habits, and hang-ups melt away.

Progress to—Heart Helps

PRIMARY PRINCIPLE: GOD TAKES DELIGHT IN YOU!

Memory Verse:
> The LORD your God is with you, he is mighty to save. He will take great delight in you, he will quiet you with his love, he will rejoice over you with singing.
>
> —Zephaniah 3:17

> **God is with you!**
> **He saves you!**
> **He takes delight in you!**
> **He sings over you!**

When my son Christopher was born, I was rocked by heartfelt emotion as I stood staring into his hospital crib. I remember telling my mother I'd never felt anything like it. I could not pick him up because a minor medical issue meant he had to stay under a bright light, so I stood by his crib to be near him. As I stood over him, stroking his velvety skin, I began to sing, "Hush little baby don't say a word. Mama's going to buy you a mocking bird."[2] My mama walked into the hospital room and began harmonizing. What a moment—mother and daughter standing there together, delightedly singing over the crib of that new, tiny wonder.

Just as Christopher delighted Mama and me, so God is even more delighted with you. He will save you and stays with you. God is so delighted that He rejoices over you with singing (Zephaniah 3:17). No matter what happens to you, if you let Him, God will quiet you with His love. That principle of pure delight will drive you to fellowship with The One who sings over you.

The Secret to Everything

Purpose: Fellowship

Discipleship → Fellowship

The purpose of loving God with your heart is joyful, playful, intimate fellowship. Discipleship, making the decision to follow Jesus (Step 1), leads to fellowship (Step 2) with Jesus. God made you for fellowship. He called you into fellowship with Jesus and with fellow believers. Fellowship with God and godly people is the secret key to victory over failure, temptations, trials, and heartbreak. It can be the joy of your existence, and it will bring delight to the heart of God.

Fellowship with Jesus

Memory Verse:

> God is faithful, by whom ye were called unto the fellowship of his Son Jesus Christ our Lord.
>
> —1 Corinthians 1:9 (KJV)

When I was five years old, my cousin Sunny moved away. He had stayed with us for a period, and I desperately missed him. Daily, I went to the window to watch for him, but he never came back. As I sat in that window, brokenhearted and staring at the beautiful Florida flowers, my loneliness lifted and I felt peace beyond description. I remember taking deep breaths and actually breathing in a peaceful feeling. God fellowshipped with me before I had the words to describe what I was experiencing. I returned to that window long after I knew Sunny was not coming home.

At eight years old, I invited Jesus into my life and began my journey of studying the Bible and learning about Jesus. It was years before I connected the feelings in that window with my intellectual belief in Jesus Christ. Eventually, my head and my heart spiritually aligned, and I deliberately began to seek daily, thrilling fellowship with Jesus. Naturally, I went back to the window.

Since my ICU experience in 1980, I've faithfully gone to a window with my Bible and journal for morning fellowship with God. I begin with a period of meditation, where I'm still and know He is God (Psalms 46:10). Then I talk, laugh, and sing with Him, pouring out my feelings, needs, and dreams. I open my Bible and stretch my mind with the empowering study of the words of God. Finally, I ask God for knowledge of His will for me and the power to carry it out. I rise from my prayer chair, knowing what I'm supposed to do and fully empowered to do it. Most days, I experience that same blissful feeling from the window of my youth.

Fellowship Stages: Desire→Discipline→Delight

Desire

Fellowship with Jesus begins with a desire to grow closer to Jesus.

- You begin longing for a deeper fellowship with God.
- Excitement builds as you prepare.
- Concern about your ability to follow through taunts you.

There is a warning for each fellowship phase. The warning for desire is that Satan will throw many roadblocks at you when you commit to greater fellowship with God.

When I first started daily fellowship with God, babies cried and washing machines overflowed. Once, a smoke detector actually went off. When I persevered no matter what, eventually Satan gave up trying to distract me.

The Secret to Everything

Discipline

Studies say only 15% of Christians have a daily discipline of time with God. My discussions with so many Americans confirm that statistic. However, I've found that the percentage of Christians who desire this discipline is much higher than 15%. Putting that desire into practice is much more difficult.

If you persevere:

- Eventually, your daily time with God becomes a habit.
- You will feel internal pressure to continue it.

The warning for this phase is that it may feel rote or even boring. You may do it because it is the right thing to do, but you may not enjoy it all the time. In the early days of my disciplined time with God, I often felt like I was talking to the walls.

Delight

Eventually desire and discipline wondrously transformed into delight, and I began waking each morning with gleeful anticipation of my time with God.

If you persist:

- You will wake up looking forward to your time with God.
- You will experience deep and rewarding fellowship.
- You will let nothing stand in your way of this time.

There is a warning to this fellowship phase. Delight has a short memory. A few skipped days of fellowship and you will lose the desire and discipline to do it. I've met many wistful Christians who say, "I used to spend time with God every day. I loved it. I don't know why I stopped."

Fellowship with Other Christians

> James, Peter and John, those reputed to be pillars, gave me and Barnabas the right hand of fellowship when they recognized the grace given to me.
>
> —Galatians 2:9

Many people I meet on the streets of America tell me that they can be spiritual and believe in Jesus without going to church. It usually causes me to gasp the words, "But why would you want to?"

True fellowship with other Christians is the closest I can get to the perfect kingdom of God while still walking around on planet earth. Since we are supposed to be the body of Christ, I think of other Christians as God with skin on. My church family teaches me, prays for me, cares for me when I'm sick, and scolds me when I need it.

I love church and long to be with other Christians. When I'm on the road as a missionary, I need fellowship, so I go to churches all across the country. Since I'm with my Christian family, I'm not a guest, and I don't act like one. I join whatever they are doing. If they go to lunch after church, I go. If it is their turn to clean up after snacks, I clean up. If they need a piano player, a teacher, or someone to set up chairs, I offer. Amazingly, even when I'm gone from home for three months, I'm never without Christian fellowship.

Promise: Understanding

Knowledge ➔ Understanding

Memory Verse:

> Through thy precepts I get understanding.
>
> —Psalm 119:104 (asv)

The Secret to Everything

Knowledge of God and the Bible leads to understanding how that knowledge applies to us. When my late son, David, was a teenager, he made choices that terrified me. We adopted him when he was six, and we grew to love him with all of our hearts. He was from an abusive home, but for several years, he blossomed; and we delighted in him. He made good grades, won piano and vocal competitions, and starred in the church Opera *Amal and the Night Visitors*. When he hit his teen years, the scars from his first six years of abuse came back to haunt him and us. I didn't understand and thought that with enough prayer, discipline, and hard work, I could fix it.

One afternoon, sitting in my window sobbing, I begged God to strike David "good." I opened my Bible and read the words of God when He was lamenting over Israel (Isaiah 30:15–18). God offered the Israelites salvation and was brokenhearted and confused about why they acted so badly when He loved them so much. God felt about Israel the same ways I did about David.

With a heaviness of heart, I finally *understood* God's gift of free will. God was God, and when the Israelites broke His heart, He could have struck them "good." Instead, He cried while He allowed them to destroy themselves. Through the knowledge of God's Word, I *understood* the painful lesson that my precious David had free will and that God would allow David to make choices that could ruin his life.

The Bible says to trust God with all your heart and never to lean on your own understanding (Proverbs 3:5). Gaining biblical knowledge by loving God with your mind leads to the godly understanding of loving God with your heart. Understanding gives you life. If you ask, God gives understanding, and understanding guards your heart against the disappointments and pain earthly life invariably offers.

Progress to—Heart Helps

> ### Understanding:
> 1. Gives Life.
> 2. Is Given by God If We Ask.
> 3. Guards Us.

Understanding Gives *Life*

> Understanding is a wellspring of life unto him that hath it.
>
> —Proverbs 16:22 (KJV)

I have felt grief so deeply that my husband had to remind me to breathe. Understanding is how we deal with grief, disappointment, anger, or any of the other many emotions that threaten to choke our breath from us. Emotions are God given. Since even Jesus wept, it isn't likely we will avoid hurtful emotions; but once we gain godly understanding, we can once again breathe in life.

God Will Give Understanding If *We Ask*

> Then he continued, "Do not be afraid, Daniel. Since the first day that you set your mind to gain understanding and to humble yourself before your God, your words were heard, and I have come in response to them."
>
> —Daniel 10:12

When my Uncle Preston understood that another of his sons was about to go to heaven, I stood next to him as he prayed, "God, I'm not going to question your will. You know best. It helped me when I understood why Bill had to die so young. I ask you now to help me understand why I'm about to lose Douglas too." That understanding allowed Uncle Preston to pass through seemingly unbearable grief that would freeze many emotionally. It was not long before Uncle Preston was laughing again and singing joyfully in his booming southern voice.

Understanding *Guards Us*

Understanding will guard you.

—Proverbs 2:11

Godly understanding is the guardian of emotions. It keeps you from going too far. If it is your turn to cry, may I suggest flat-out wailing? Then, allow God to help you to recover. Even though circumstances whirl around you, you won't lose heart because God will renew your heart day by day (2 Corinthians 4:16).

Process

Four-Step Fellowship Process

As I said, since 1980 and my ICU waiting room experience, I've been waking up each morning to fellowship with God. I never again want to be without the emotional connection of spiritual fellowship. Normally, I spend about thirty minutes with God and my Bible. When I'm overworked or under stress, I double and triple my morning time with God. Below is the process I use for my daily fellowship with God.

1. Meditation (5 Minutes)

My meditation of him shall be sweet.

—Psalm 104:34 (KJV)

Many Christians are wary about meditation because the practice is so popular among non-Christian religions. Non-Christian religions do not have the exclusive claim on meditation. The word "meditation" is in the Bible many times, and as Christians, we cheat our personal relationship with God if we skip this biblical practice of calming our minds, focusing on God, and listening to His voice. Meditation is listening to the voice of God.

Below is a partial Biblical list for meditational focus:

- Promises (Psalm 119:148)
- Law (Psalm 119:97)
- Love (Psalm 48:9)
- Works (Psalm 143:5)
- Wonders (Psalm 119:27)
- Precepts (Psalm 119:15)

2. Prayer (5–10 minutes)—The Five P's of Prayer

But you, dear friends, build yourselves up in your most holy faith and pray in the Holy Spirit.

—Jude 20

If mediation is listening to God, prayer is talking with Him. The Bible says to pray in the morning, at night before we go to sleep, and without ceasing. In other words, we are to be in a constant state of prayer. The five P's of prayer is the simple prayer guide I created for my morning time with God. I do this with a pen and journal.

> ### The Five P's of Prayer
>
> - **Plan**—Ask God for wisdom and list your plans for the day.
> - **Praise**—List your blessings and joys.
> - **Pain**—Tell God your problems, what hurts, and your concerns.
> - **Petition**—Ask God for the desires of your heart.
> - **Profession**—Confess your mistakes, unholy desires, and wayward thoughts from the day before and make your commitments for the new day.

3. Bible Study (10–20 Minutes)

> For everything that was written in the past was written to teach us, so that through endurance and the encouragement of the Scriptures we might have hope.
>
> —Romans 15:4

The Bible is the Word of God. Think of the wonder of that. You can open a book and hear *God* talking to you. Step 1 established that the secret to having the mind of Christ is Bible Study and that the secret to good self-esteem and success is having the mind of Christ. You can wake up every morning and suit up with God's armor (Ephesians 6:13–18). You can tuck your shirt into the belt of truth and strap on your thigh-pads of righteousness. You can slip in to your cross-trainers that provide the preparation of the gospel of peace; grab your shield of faith; and put on your protective headgear, the helmet of salvation. The Word of God is your only offensive weapon against the evils of the world. Why would anyone ever consider leaving home in the morning without arming him or herself with words from God? Bible study is different from just meditating on a scripture. It is taking the scripture apart, looking at the context and history, and praying to understand what it means for you today. There are many ways to study the Bible and tools with which to study it. The important thing is to study the Bible daily.

4. Application (5 Minutes)

Then said he, Lo, I come to do thy will, O God.

—Hebrews 10:9 (KJV)

We've listened, talked, read God's words, and have only just begun. All the meditation, prayer, and Bible study in the world is useless unless you leave your closeted time with God, apply His Word, and do His will. God's Word and your faith will only merge when you obey and apply it to your life. Suggestions for ending your morning time with God are:

- Ask God for knowledge of His will for you and the power to carry it out.
- Spend a few minutes journaling what you learned, felt, and heard.
- Write specifically what you've heard God say for you to do and check it off when you've done it.
- Check what you've learned, felt, and heard against the Bible (God will never act contrary to His Word).
- Stand up empowered to walk out into the world and bravely obey the voice God.

As you go through your day, if you experience doubt or anxiety, get alone with God and affirm what you heard Him say to do.

The Secret to Everything

Problems: Yes, But...

Here we go again. Those famous words, "Yes, but," threaten to trip us and send us tumbling down into the mire. Maybe your "Yes, buts" sound a little like mine.

Yes, But I Like to Wallow in My Emotions

Admit it. Wallowing is fun. After all, aren't your feelings justified? Maybe someone hurt you or treated you unfairly. You probably think you deserve better, but alas, life isn't fair. After all, Jesus died on the cross. Certainly, He deserved better. *So,* instead of wallowing:

- Practice forgiveness: "Then said Jesus, Father, forgive them; for they know not what they do" (Luke 23:34 KJV).
- Use the Serenity Prayer: "God grant me the serenity to accept the things I cannot change, the courage to change the things I can, and the wisdom to know the difference."[3]

Yes, But I'm Upset (Worried, Angry, Tired, Lonely...) All the Time

But the fruit of the Spirit is love, joy, peace, patience, kindness, goodness, faithfulness, gentleness and self-control.

—Galatians 5:22–23

Stress is hard on the heart. My husband, Bob, once went through job-related stress that affected his mood at home. Unfortunately, I briefly let his stress become mine, and the fruits of my spirit rotted on the vine and plopped to the ground. I summoned Bob, and he and I had another of those dreaded talks. Then I took a day off to run errands and focus my eyes back on Jesus.

It worked. In less than four hours, I could taste sweet fruit. I called Bob and said, "My fruit is blooming again. If you're going to mess with my fruit, I'm going to run more errands."

He laughed and said, "It's safe to come home. My fruit is blooming again too."

Since that day, our running joke has been, "Don't mess with my fruit."

Are people or circumstances messing with your fruit? How you feel does not have to depend on circumstances. If you are constantly upset, angry, tired, or worried, you are probably not experiencing the sweet nectar of the fruit of the Spirit. Here are some ideas for breaking the cycle:

- Take a break and spend time with God.
- Choose happiness regardless of your circumstances (Abraham Lincoln once said, "People are about as happy as they make up their minds to be).[4]
- Ask God to send you His fruit.
- Make a gratitude list and praise God.

Yes, But Mood Swings Make Me Interesting

Tell him, "Listen, calm down."

—Isaiah 7:4 (The Message)

Take God's words to Isaiah to heart. Listen and calm down. Mood swings may be interesting, but the motion sickness that comes from living life on an emotional roller coaster is dangerous for the heart. Things to remember about mood swings are:

- You may be the only one who thinks they are interesting.
- Mood swings are contagious and take others on the nasty roller coaster ride.

- Practicing meditation helps.
- Taking care of spiritual and biological needs (including sexual, if you are married) is critical.
- Medical help may be necessary.
- Relaxation and play are the best medicine.
- The Fruit of the Spirit (Galatians 5:22–23) is always available to us.

Yes, But It Really Was Personal

Keep us forgiven with you and forgiving others.

—Matthew 6:12 (The Message)

Sometimes what others do to us or say about us really is personal. You may have heard the expression, "What other people think about me is none of my business." That may be true, but finding out people do not like us is hard on the ego. Imagine how the human Jesus felt when people hated him so badly they crucified Him. Do you remember what he said? "Father, forgive them, for they do not know what they are doing" (Luke 23:34 NIV).

When people hurt you:

- Get over it.
- Practice offering grace.
- Ask God for understanding.
- Pray, "Father forgive them, they don't know what they are doing."

Yes, But People Run When They See Me Coming

A merry heart maketh a cheerful countenance but by sorrow of the heart the spirit is broken.

—Proverbs 15:13 (KJV)

Progress to—Heart Helps

Does the party stop when you enter a room? Recently I heard a grieving mother discussing the tragic death of her daughter. One icy night, after picking up her young sons from a friend's home, her daughter lost control of the car. My friend's two grandsons were seriously injured, and her daughter was killed. This brokenhearted mother and grandmother said, "The party started when my daughter entered the room. Now, I feel like the party stops when I enter a room."

It was my girlfriend's time to mourn. Her heart was broken, but what I know from experience is that if she allows it, her merry heart will return. She was and will be again very much like her merry-hearted beautiful daughter, and the party will one day start when she enters a room.

Mourning isn't a sin or a weakness, and merriness isn't frivolous. They are both seasons that most pass through many times during life. When it is your turn to be merry:

- Take your turn.
- Cheer up.
- Smile when you see people coming.
- Speak affirmations instead of criticizing or complaining.

Yes, But The Church Hurt My Feelings

> Let us not give up meeting together, as some are in the habit of doing, but let us encourage one another.
>
> —Hebrews 10:25

When I mention I am a Christian, many feel obligated to report their church horror stories to me. Nightmarish tales of gossip, meanness, promiscuity, back stabbing, abuse, theft, and fighting are so hauntingly familiar that I occasionally wonder if people are just passing the same stories around. I listen, apologize on behalf of the church, and gently remind them that the Bible says to go to church. Church is family, and families make mistakes. My suggestions for dealing with church sins are:

- Forgive the church.
- Stop expecting the church to be perfect.
- Be a part of the solution instead of the problem.
- Don't take things personally.
- Be faithful with your attendance.
- If the problems are sufficiently serious and insurmountable, change churches.

Yes, But I'm Grieving, and I Can't Get Over It

There is a time for everything and a season for every activity under heaven: A time to be born and a time to die, a time to plant and a time to uproot, a time to kill and a time to heal, a time to tear down and a time to build, a time to weep and a time to laugh, a time to mourn and a time to dance, a time to scatter stones and a time to gather them, a time to embrace and a time to refrain, a time to search and a time to give up, a time to keep and a time to throw away, a time to tear and a time to mend, a time to be silent and a time to speak, a time to love and a time to hate, a time for war and a time for peace.

—Ecclesiastes 3:2–8

I meet so many people with broken hearts. It's as if they have just lost heart for anything other than the grief they are feeling. It is hard to love God with a broken heart, and the only answer is to let Him quiet us with His love. When we allow The Great Comforter to comfort us, our hearts heal, and we are able to love God with a whole and healthy heart. Here's a process that I have found to be useful:

- Identify the season you are in.

Progress to—Heart Helps

- Accept it and experience it fully. If it is your turn to mourn, wail. If it is your turn to laugh, laugh with the abandonment of a child.
- Whether easy or difficult, let each season pass by, allowing God to quiet you with His love.
- Gracefully and courageously move to the next season, even if it is difficult.

Yes, But I Need a Vacation

> By the seventh day God had finished the work he had been doing; so on the seventh day he rested from all his work.
>
> —Genesis 2:2–3

Our hearts need a break. God demonstrated our need for rest by resting Himself on the seventh day. If you think you need time off, you probably do. So:

- Take a vacation.
- Plan regular rest periods—weekly, monthly, and yearly.
- Learn to play.

PRACTICAL APPLICATIONS

My life and travel experiences offer many training opportunities. Some of them I appreciate at the time. All of them I appreciate *in* time. In this section, I'll share a few.

Would You Give It Back?

When my son David died at age twenty-six, I thought my heart would break. I was not angry, but I was achingly sad. I could not blame God because I knew the mistakes David made had caused his death. It is no wonder that he died of AIDS. I decided not to blame David because God gave me the grace to offer David grace in spite of the fact that David's actions took him away from me.

What made his death particularly heart wrenching was that for his last year in this world, he turned his life around. David told us that while standing on top of an ocean-side cliff in Maui, God sent him a vision about dying. David was already quite sick. David said God gave him a glimpse of heaven and said not to be afraid. He said that God told him to make the most of the rest of his life. David climbed down the bluff and called home for the first time in two years. My son Christopher and I immediately flew to Hawaii to visit.

David lived for one more year after we reestablished a family connection and died clean and sober. He had a good job, and the only debts he left were the deductibles from his last hospital stay. He had an apartment that overlooked Waikiki Bay and a host of emotionally healthy friends. David called home several times a week and gave memorable gifts for each holiday and birthday. In short, we got a glimpse of what loving an emotionally healthy David would be like. It hurt to say "goodbye."

When Bob and I were in Hawaii making David's final arrangements, a man offered his condolences. He said, "I'm so sorry for your loss. I understand. I've lost two sons. The pain does get easier."

"How can you bear it?" I gasped, hoping to hear a secret.

"If God offered you a wonderful gift for twenty-six years, would you refuse it because you knew you would have to give it back?"

"I guess not," I muttered warily.

"That's how I stand it," he said. "I think of the time I had with my boys as a gift. Who am I to argue when my time with the gift was over? My boys were from God to begin with. I'm grateful for the time I had them."

Thinking of the time I had with David as a gift was what helped me grieve the loss and pass to the next season. I would not have refused the gift, even if God had told me beforehand that I'd have to give it back.

Lighten Up

Years ago, people continually told me to "lighten up." Finally, I asked a mentor what they meant. She said, "Cheryle, you are always so serious. Do you ever read books just for fun?"

Guiltily, I remembered all the religious and self-help books I'd read over the last months.

"Do you ever play?" she asked.

"Well," I said, "I play Bridge and Pinochle."

She laughed. "Not what I meant. I'm talking about laughing, jumping, running, and twirling. I'm talking about playing with abandonment and falling into a heap of giggles."

"Well," I muttered, "I laugh at television sitcoms."

She sighed. "I have two suggestions for you. Buy a fun novel, and ask a fun child to teach you how to play."

Thus began my romance with romance novels. In my defense, I do not read trash. But the books I read offer no great lasting literary value. They are just for fun.

I also went to my then four-year-old nephew Jim and asked, "Would you teach me to play?"

"Yes, Aunt Cheryle," he said excitedly. "It's easy."

For the next few months, Jim and I dashed through toy stores, touching everything. He picked out my first toy collection and showed me how to use it. I followed Jim through bounce houses, rooms filled with tiny balls, and zoos. We picked up worms, caught fish, and played in the muddy shores of my lake. I've always been a quick study and took to playing like a monkey takes to monkey bars—in fact, I even learned about monkey bars myself.

Now I'm like Peter Pan, who never grew up. Many children have grown up and left me, but I'm still quite comfortable

The Secret to Everything

blowing bubbles and balancing on a curb as I walk down the street. My toy collection would rival any modern day child's, and I have two zoo memberships and an annual pass to an amusement park.

I haven't heard the expression "lighten up" in years because I, indeed, have lightened up. I know what the Bible means when it says to let my heart be merry. Jesus said that a little child would lead us, and Jim certainly led me. Jesus also said that unless we receive the kingdom like a little child, we won't enter it (Mark 10:15). I plan to dance my way into the kingdom.

Points to Ponder

Can you imagine the majestic God that created the heavens and earth singing over you? What must it sound like? I once heard Pavarotti sing in Carnegie Hall. Pavarotti was the most famous tenor in the world. When he sang, he touched hearts, and audiences wept. As wonderful as Pavarotti sang, I'm sure God is better.

When you understand that God is so delighted with you that He sings over you, you can surrender to the various seasons of your life without losing heart, giving up, or ending up stuck in a season. When you finally let God quiet your heart with His love and then bask in that love, you will be ready to love Him with a whole and healthy heart.

Step 3

Progress to—
Soul Soothers

And thou shalt love the Lord thy God with all thy soul.

—Mark 12:30

Mind → Heart → Soul

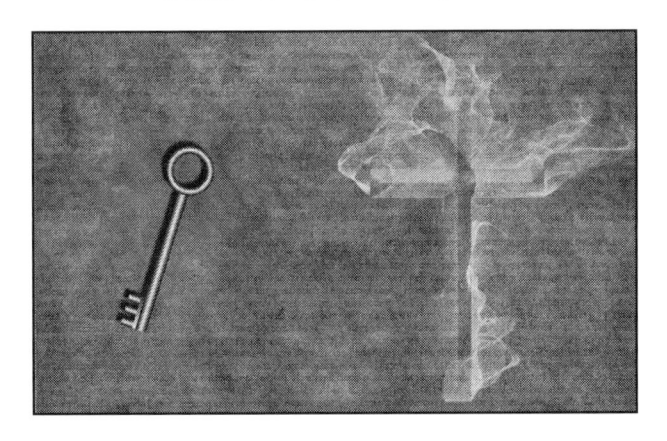

AFTER MY GRANDFATHER'S funeral, I thought back to my phone booth experience. I had asked God for help, and He had majestically answered my prayer. I'd prepared for that moment by spending the previous year putting down the false gods in my life and by reaching out to others through something as mundane as quarters. Suddenly, I understood the power that comes from serving a risen Jesus, who can do anything. I understood how my grandparents could continue to function and be happy when their hearts were breaking. I never wanted to find myself without that Power again.

I made some personal commitments. Before that experience, my personal prayer life and Bible Study were guilt driven, undisciplined, and full of stops and starts. I decided I would begin each day with meditation, prayer, and Bible Study. I ended each session with a prayer that asked God for knowledge of His will for me and the power to carry it out. I began the daily practice of worshipping the God I would be spending my eternity with. I left those quiet times committed to acting on what God revealed during those precious, intimate moments together. Through that intimate time with God, I began to truly know myself.

Do you know yourself? People have struggled to know themselves throughout history. Etched into the forecourt of the ancient Greek Temple of Apollo at Delphi was the famous aphorism, "Know Thyself." Perhaps the reason we struggle so hard to know ourselves is that we want to discover what we really want. If we truly knew what we wanted, perhaps we would eliminate that vague sense of restlessness, craving, and dissatisfaction driving others and us to distraction. Maybe the quest to know ourselves is really a search for the illusive obsession we call "happiness."

> **Loving God with your entire soul is the secret to never-ending joy.**

Happiness comes and goes, depending on circumstances. That nameless feeling that makes us constantly seek more, something different, or attention is a need to fill hollow souls.

Progress to—Soul Soothers

The secret to filling that emptiness or scratching that itch is for our souls to embrace God's Spirit. That's why I believe that loving God with our entire souls is the secret to neverending joy. Focusing all energy on loving God with our entire souls is the secret to unlocking our souls and having the promised peace and joy that is beyond our ability to understand.

Your soul is the essence of who you are and has an eternal life span. When the original disciples met the risen Jesus, their fears evaporated and they went boldly into the dangerous world of sharing their faith. Like the disciples, when you come face to face with the risen Lord, you embrace Him as your soul connects with Jesus' Spirit. His purpose becomes yours and launches you into action. Gone are your sense of confusion. Gone are your trembling, restlessness, and doubt. You can identify and rebuke strongholds, those hurts, habits, and hang ups that keep you from worshipping the one true God. You will become like soldiers on a mission to save their country, mothers rescuing endangered children, or mountain lions stalking prey. The risen Lord's power becomes yours, and nothing can stand in the way of your fulfilling God's call on your life. When you finally love God with your entire soul, life struggles lose their power, and you begin eternal worship of the one true God while you are still on this earth. Learning to love God with your entire soul is pivotal in your spiritual walk and empowers you to become the person God wants. Your quest for happiness vaporizes, and instead, you will have learned the secret to contentment in all of your circumstances.

PRIMARY PRINCIPLE: JESUS ROSE FROM THE DEAD!

Memory Verse:

You are looking for Jesus the Nazarene, who was crucified. He has risen!

—Mark 16:6

The Secret to Everything

The primary principle of Step 3 is that you serve a risen Lord. When you understand the dynamic power of the resurrection, embracing God, soul to Spirit is easy. Unfortunately, many Christians still serve a crucified Jesus.

Usually when I picked my daughter Kelley up from four-year-old preschool, she bounced into the car, blond ringlets swinging, babbling about the events of the morning. The Thursday before Easter, she opened the car door and burst into tears. "Mommy," she sobbed. "They *killed* Him. They *killed* Him. He's dead."

"Kelley," I said, horrified. "Who are you talking about? *Who* did they kill?"

"Jesus," she said. "They killed him and hung him on a cross." Her shoulders were shaking as she wailed.

Her teacher had given gory details of the Easter story, and I was not thrilled. Up to that point, Kelley's Bible studies had included stories about love, animals, healings, and hope. I hadn't gotten around to death and mayhem and certainly not the gruesome details of what humans did to Jesus. As I experienced the pain of the crucifixion through the eyes of my brokenhearted daughter, I realized she'd heard only part of the story. The teacher may have explained the rest, but my tenderhearted darling with the spiritual gift of mercy would not have heard anything beyond nails, blood, and crosses.

"*Kelley!*" I said excitedly. "Look at me. Jesus *rose* from the dead! He didn't stay on the cross. He was so powerful that He came back to life. Jesus is alive!"

"He…he… is?" she said hopefully between hiccups.

"Yes, sweetie," I said. "He came back to life."

Historical facts confirm the crucifixion of Jesus Christ, and many non-Christians accept the crucifixion. For them, Jesus existed but died on the cross. He had no power to overcome death. Unfortunately, many Christians also succumb to this notion and find themselves looking for a crucified Lord to solve their problems. They believe in and love Jesus for dying for them, and may even offer lip service to the resurrection, but they fail at believing in Jesus' resurrection power to handle their seemingly impossible situations.

In Dodge City, Kansas, I met a college student full of the intellectual vim and vigor that drives the young. I'm a fan of the long ago television show *Gunsmoke,* so I was enjoying the Boot Hill Museum and the staged gunfights that mimicked the show's theme. It was hard to take this young cowboy seriously because he was one of the actors dressed in the historical western garb, complete with chaps, low hanging pistols, and a whip.

"Are you a Christian?" I asked.

"I go to church and believe in Jesus and God," he drawled. "I don't much buy that He rose from the dead."

"God wouldn't be much of a God if He couldn't overcome death," I teased.

"I hadn't thought about that. You're right," the stunned boy said.

"Your Savior will be more powerful when you meet the risen Lord," I promised.

We may say the words, "He is alive," but our futile efforts to control our temporal lives demonstrate our hesitancy to look beyond that short-lived, crucified state of our Lord. When the world crucified Jesus, the disciples' hearts were broken, and they trembled and hid in fear. At one point, Peter even denied knowing Christ, thus denying His love. Like those formerly cowardly disciples who loved Jesus with their minds when they followed this amazing teacher and had their hearts broken when the world crucified Him, maybe we have not reached the point in our spiritual journeys where our souls are truly intimate with the risen Lord.

When the disciples met the risen Lord, their souls embraced His Spirit, and they began an eternity of worshipping the risen Lord. When they understood the power of the resurrection, they left their hiding places and gained the wisdom to know what to do next.

When you kiss the face of the risen Lord, nothing He asks is too much, and you really can do all things through Christ who strengthens you (Philippians 4:17).

Purpose: Worship

Discipleship → Fellowship → Worship

Memory Verse:

> Worship the Lord in the splendor of his holiness; tremble before him, all the earth.
>
> —Psalm 96:9

The purpose of loving God with all your soul is to worship Him now and for all eternity. The question is not if you worship, it is what or whom you worship. You *will* worship something. God created humankind with an instinctive desire to worship. Civilizations have always sought and/or built objects of worships. Unfortunately, need for worship combined with a lack of faith in the One who created the need to worship causes people to create objects of their desires. Often those poor worship substitutes grip lives and turn into strongholds that ruin lives. There is a God-shaped hole in everyone that demands to be filled. If you do not fill that hole with what truly fits, you will continually stuff that hole with harmful substances and actions. When you worship God in the splendor of His holiness, everything else becomes lack luster.

Becoming a disciple of Jesus is the first step to meeting your need to worship. The fellowship discussed in Step 2 follows discipleship as you fall in love with Jesus with your heart. True fellowship with the risen Jesus propels your soul to worship the one true God in the "splendor of His holiness." In Step 3, your need for worship substitutes melts away when your soul is finally satisfied. When you love God with all your soul, worship is the natural outpouring of that love.

God is holy and worthy of our worship. There may be no biblical definition of worship, but there are certainly plenty of biblical examples. American churches have found a way to use all of them as well as make up some. In my journeys, I've worshipped with those who knelt, raised hands, sang, clapped, twirled, and cheered. Some danced in the aisles, and others prayed for those who danced. I've witnessed people using dogs, snakes, tambourines, fire, smoke, fog, and toys as worship props. I'll admit to being uncomfortable with many worship practices I've witnessed, and some I strongly disagreed with. I want the focus of my worship to always be on God.

Worship is personal and takes on many different forms. God commands you to worship with believers in church. Worship can be anywhere, anytime. I personally have been known to worship God in the car, in malls, and even during an IRS tax audit. When you love God with all your soul, God will unlock your soul so that you can worship at the feet of Jesus and praise Him in all things.

PROMISE: WISDOM

Knowledge → Understanding → Wisdom

Memory Verse:

He who gets wisdom loves his own soul.

—Proverbs 19:8

Do you love your own soul? The last step in this five-step-process is loving your neighbor as yourself. To get to that point, you must first

The Secret to Everything

love yourself. Your soul is the essence of "you." The secret to loving your soul is gaining God's wisdom (Proverbs 19:8). When you take Step 3 to heart and unlock your soul from a self-imposed prison, poor self-esteem will vanish as you begin to love your own soul. You will learn, become, and love who God created you to be. Knowledge will have led to understanding and understanding to wisdom. As you gain God's wisdom, you can become willing to trust Him with everything as you understand His love and power in relationship to your circumstances. That godly wisdom will allow you to become the amazing person God envisioned. God's wisdom is simple to receive:

Secret Wisdom Formula

1. **Ask.**
2. **Believe without doubt.**

Ask

> If any of you lacks wisdom, he should ask God, who gives generously to all without finding fault, and it will be given to him.
>
> —James 1:5–6

Wisdom is always available if you ask. God is generous, and James 1:5 says He gives it to all who ask. What part of *all* is not clear? Godly wisdom is recognizable because it builds on knowledge of what the Bible says about circumstances and understanding of how that applies to your life.

Believe Without Doubt

> But when he asks, he must believe and not doubt, because he who doubts is like a wave of the sea, blown and tossed by the wind.
>
> —James 1:6–7

Progress to—Soul Soothers

Belief is where most of us stumble. Lack of belief causes disobedience. After you ask, you must believe, act immediately, and not doubt or you'll get seasick. Who wants to be blown and tossed about like a wave in the sea?

Process

Loving God with your entire soul starts with ridding your soul of God substitutes. That includes false idols like power or money; strongholds like overeating, drugs, or alcohol; and obsessive attachments to people. You need to give up control of everything in your life and surrender your soul to God. As discussed in previous chapters, steps to getting to this point are discipleship and daily fellowship with God and other Christians. Resources to maintain our commitment include immersion in church, Bible study, support groups, time with mentors, and counseling. You can love God with your entire soul by applying these three simple statements…

Loving God With Your Soul Means Saying:

- **I Can't!**
- **God Can!**
- **I Think I'll Let Him!**

I Can't!

> For troubles without number surround me; my sins have overtaken me, and I cannot see. They are more than the hairs of my head, and my heart fails within me.
>
> —Psalm 40:12

The Secret to Everything

You wail the words, "Nobody knows the trouble I've seen," to anyone who will listen. You long to control everyone you love and everything you care about so that the trouble will go away.

For many of you, if you were God, you would eliminate free will and make it a rule that everyone behave the way that makes you feel the best. You'd hold all of those troubles at bay and orchestrate a happy ending to every story. Every once in the while, circumstances may tease you and lead you to believe that you have some control, but then something happens that dashes your hopes and makes you realize how powerless you really are. When you finally surrender to your powerlessness over people and circumstances, you realize with a sense of relief that you are not God and do not have the weight of the world resting on your shoulders.

God Can!

> Let the morning bring me word of your unfailing love, for I have put my trust in you.
>
> —Psalm 143:8a

Why is it so hard to remember that God can do anything? If you serve a risen Lord, surely you'll realize the power it took to overcome death and be willing to join the Psalmist in saying, "I have put my trust in You" (Psalm 143:8). Since God was willing to be tortured and die for you, He must have your best interests at heart.

So what is the problem? The problem is that you may be living as if your God is still crucified and you don't really believe He can manage the world without your help. What a relief it is to meet the risen Lord and grasp that regardless of your ability to see how, God can work everything out for your good if you love Him (Romans 8:28).

Progress to—Soul Soothers

I Think I'll Let Him!

> Show me the way I should go, for to you I lift up my soul.
>
> —Psalm 143:8b

Now comes the hard part. You can unlock your soul by letting go and letting God have control of everything in your life. What a concept. You can stop demanding outcomes and trust that all things really are working together for your good. You can accept the responsibility that you can do all things through Christ and say "yes" to anything God tells you to do. You can lay your idols and strongholds on God's altar and set a match to them. You can let God remove everything in your life that is hampering your ability or desire to love God with your entire soul. Then you can discover the secret to this step. You thought surrender was the hard part, but the secret is that surrender is really the easy part. You can take a deep breath and feel untouchable as you begin soaring through your life as if on eagle's wings.

Problems: Yes, But…

Yes, but we are back to those pesky "Yes, buts." The journey of loving God with your entire soul could start to feel as if you are losing yourself, which may trigger all kinds of dangerous defense mechanisms that must be ignored.

Yes, But I Don't Know Who I Am

> We have different gifts, according to the grace given us. If a man's gift is prophesying, let him use it in proportion to his faith. If it is serving, let him serve; if it is teaching, let him teach; if it is encouraging, let him encourage; if it is contributing to the needs of others, let him give generously; if it is leadership, let him govern diligently; if it is showing mercy, let him do it cheerfully.
>
> —Romans 12:6–8

The Secret to Everything

Everywhere, I meet people struggling to know who they are. They joke, "I'm still trying to figure out who I want to be when I grow up." In the light of all eternity, it doesn't really matter who we are. What matters is who we can become. The gifts listed in Romans 12:6–8 are often nicknamed the personality gifts because they describe seven basic personality traits. That scripture is my favorite personality test. Most people, believers and non-believers, naturally fall heavily into one or two of these seven personality types. Children are born with these traits dominant in their lives. One child naturally wants to help and the other wants to boss everyone around. Jesus demonstrated all seven of these gifts, and since we can grow up to be Christ-like, we can mature in all areas. Regardless of the traits we were born with, we can become more like Christ.

Suggestions for becoming who God intends you to be are:

- Identify your spiritual gifts.
- Identify your passions.
- Ask God to show you how to combine your passions with your spiritual gifts for kingdom use.
- Ask God to help you improve the areas where you are the weakest.
- Do what God says.

Yes, But I'm Unhappy With My:

- **Institutions:** church, employer, and/or the government.
- **Relationships:** spouse, family, friends, and/or God.

I know what it is to be in need, and I know what it is to have plenty. I have learned the secret of being content in any and every situation, whether well fed or hungry, whether living in plenty or in want. I can do everything through him who gives me strength.

—Philippians 4:12–13

Progress to—Soul Soothers

The above statement is a quote from the famous author and apostle Paul. We don't know his last name, but we know plenty about his circumstances. He was both wealthy and poor over the course of his life. He was beaten, chained, and jailed. If he could find contentment in all circumstances, anyone could. The secret to contentment that Paul discovered was that he could do everything through the one who gave him strength.

I could have just as easily written that statement, because I know what it is to be in need and I know what it is to have plenty. Occasionally, life on the road grows wearisome. At one campground, the outdoor shower reminded me of a scene from the famous Beverley Hillbilly's home before that bubbling crude came up from the ground.[5] It was freezing, and the shower had a barrel around it that covered me from my neck to my ankles. I had to pull a string that dumped cold water onto my shivering head. As I rushed through the shower, I worried about a tall basketball player walking by and peeking down at my shivering body. I prayed, *God, what am I doing here when I have five heated showers at home?*

His still small voice whispered, "*You are being obedient.*"

I've had to learn to be content travelling thousands of miles from my family, sleeping in tents, doing without showers, and eating food with bugs in it. Loving God with my entire soul enables me to be content in all circumstances. Below are some suggestions for being content:

- Go to your church, work, family, and friend gatherings and have fun.
- Pay your taxes.
- Comply with policies, procedures, and government regulations.
- Do your best.
- Stop whining.
- Thank God for everything.

The Secret to Everything

Yes, But I Can't Stop (Overeating, Drinking, Using, Playing, Reading…)

> When you sit to dine with a ruler, note well what is before you, and put a knife to your throat if you are given to gluttony. Do not crave his delicacies, for that food is deceptive. Do not wear yourself out to get rich; have the wisdom to show restraint.
>
> —Proverbs 23:1–4

Strongholds like addictions and obsessions may be the single most powerful tool of Satan for cutting a soul off from experiencing the presence of God. Christians and non-Christians suffer from them. I've come to recognize the ravages of the various strongholds. I've developed a theory that people even come to look like their stronghold. An alcoholic face puffs up like the puffs of grain used to make alcohol. Drug addicts' stick-like bodies resemble the needles they stick in their arms. Gluttons become as lumpy and bumpy as the pastries they gorge on. The stronghold of bitterness molds a face into an angry, lined marble statue. The difficulty with strongholds is they lie by whispering that there is no hope of ever overcoming them. Below is a partial list of strongholds:

- **Pleasure**: money, sex, entertainment
- **Power**: fame, fortune, control
- **Addictions**: food, drugs, alcohol, gambling
- **Relationships**: romance, children, family, friends

For some, when they asked, God instantly removed all desire for the stronghold. More often, though, those caught in a stronghold have to rely completely on God, live life one day at a time, and work hard to resist daily temptation. Tips for releasing strongholds are:

- Identify the stronghold.

Progress to—Soul Soothers

- Learn what the Bible says about the stronghold.
- Rebuke Satan by speaking Scripture aloud.
- Stop ungodly behavior.
- Confess behavior to God, yourself, and a trusted friend or spiritual advisor.
- Ask God to remove your desire for the stronghold.
- Make amends to anyone you've hurt.
- Accept grace and quit blaming yourself.
- Persevere no matter what.
- Get immediate supplemental help: Twelve-Step Programs, classes, church groups, counseling, and/or mentoring.
- Remember:
  - Our Savior rose from the dead!
  - Worshiping anything else is a poor substitute.
  - Removing this stronghold is child's play for a risen Savior.

Yes, But God Might Send Me to Africa as a Missionary

If they obey and serve him, they will spend the rest of their days in prosperity and their years in contentment.

—Job 36:11

God might send you to Africa. After all, He called me to leave a high six-figure salary and go on the road as a missionary. It may be God's idea of a practical joke that He teased me with five-star hotels and then stuck me in campgrounds. I've had a mountain lion and an evil man stalk me, and I've awakened surrounded by alligators and coyotes. I get lonely, discouraged, and even angry while I'm traveling. I've been in snow storms, hurricanes, wind storms, monsoons, and sand storms during my treks through all fifty states. I've broken down in most states. In walking trails, I've stumbled upon bears, snakes, spiders, and a bobcat.

The Secret to Everything

Here is the thing about Africa or campgrounds. If God really wants you in Africa or campgrounds, you will not be content or prosperous anywhere else (Job 36:11). As an example, I adore holding my grandchildren. Feeling their arms around my neck and their soft skin on my face is the closest to contentment I could feel on my own. Yet, it is not as wonderful as picking bugs from my food while I am in a campground doing God's will. I'll admit that heaven on earth is holding my grandchildren during the time God allots for that, but it is second to being where God sends me. Loving God with all our souls offers us the desire and ability to spend our days in the contentment and prosperity of resting in God's arms.

- Allow your Savior to get down from the cross.
- Look into the eyes of the risen Lord.
- Ask for knowledge of God's will for you and the power to carry it out.
- Check what you hear against the Word of God.
- Take a breath, and do what God tells you to do!

Yes, But I Feel Like I'm Wandering Aimlessly Through Life

> And we know that in all things God works for the good of those who love him, who have been called according to his purpose.
>
> —Romans 8:28–29

If you feel like you are bouncing like a ping-pong ball from random circumstance to circumstance, you may be right. You may have heard that God works everything out for good. That is a partial quote of Romans 8:28 from the Bible. Read the entire statement. He works things out for good if we love Him and if we live according to His purpose. The *Sh'ma* tells us that loving

Progress to—Soul Soothers

Him means each of us must love Him with his or her entire mind, heart, soul, and strength.

Do you remember the easy wisdom formula? We ask and believe:

- Ask God for wisdom.
- Check the wisdom you think you hear with what the Bible says about it.
- Believe God answered, and trust your instincts.
- Act without doubt.
- Look for the good in all circumstances.

Yes, But Church is (Disappointing, Frustrating, Boring…)

> The church, you see, is not peripheral to the world; the world is peripheral to the church.
>
> —Ephesians 1:23 (The Message)

I've lost track of the number of church horror stories I've heard across America. I listen sympathetically, shudder, apologize on behalf of the church, and then encourage them to get right back on the proverbial horse. Church is not a choice. It is a command. The church is not peripheral to the world. It is the other way around. Everything in the world revolves around the church. We must go.

- Understand that the rest of your life is peripheral to the church and if that relationship isn't right, all other relationships will prove difficult.
- Proceed cautiously and prayerfully if you are considering a church change. Changing churches is the equivalent to changing families and is disruptive for years and perhaps generations to come.

- Develop the attitude that worship is for God and not for you.
- Put aside personal preferences for the good of reaching people who need Christ and unity through your church family.
- Be faithful.
- Be productive.

Yes, But I Don't Need Church Because I Can Worship Anywhere

> The church is Christ's body, in which he speaks and acts, by which he fills everything with his presence.
>
> —Ephesians 1:23 (The Message)

Several times a week, people tell me that they don't need church. I just sigh because I know what they mean. I too worship on top of mountains, by oceans, and even when broken down beside the road. At one time, I thought that was enough, but I was wrong. The problem is that if we do not go to church, we miss part of how Christ speaks and acts in the world. We miss the astounding experience of how God fills everything with His presence though church. We can't explain it, but if we have experienced it, we never forget it.

- You can and should worship everywhere, but God commands you to go to church.
- The church is Christ's body.
- Christ speaks, acts, and fills you with His presence through the church!
- If you are not there, you'll miss what He reveals through the church.

Progress to—Soul Soothers

Practical Applications

Powerless Over a Cookie?

It was just a cookie—a tiny morsel of flour, eggs, and sugar. Surely, the eggs could count as a protein serving. The Bible says flour is good. How can one little cookie be more powerful than any will power I could muster? I still don't know the answer to that, but I do know it was true.

The strongholds of cookies, cakes, fried chicken, and the like almost killed me. By the time I was twenty-six, I was grossly obese and suffering from many weight-related health problems. I spent most of my days in bed, eating and letting my sweet mama care for my children. My career was nonexistent, and loved ones fretted, prayed, and lectured me. I went on diets repeatedly and all of them worked—until I stopped dieting and went back to gorging. I was a Christian practicing gluttony trapped in the jaws of a debilitating, life-destroying stronghold. No matter how hard I tried to stop, I just kept right on eating.

On January 19, 1979, thirty years to the day that I found myself writing this paragraph, I surrendered that stronghold to God. He and I made a deal. I agreed to put down every unnecessary and tempting food choice. I agreed to participate in a support group to help remind me of my commitment. I'd do my best to carry out what God told me to do every day. God's part was to remove the stronghold and reveal His will. I've mostly kept my vow, and God has more than kept His.

What an amazing journey I have had. God restored my health. I went back to school and got a Master's in Business Administration. The dying woman who spent her days in bed suddenly was running a successful software company and occasionally dining with national politicians. The sick woman who was a drain on church resources became a trusted contributing member of the body of Christ. Two generations of family members have no memory of Cheryle the practicing glutton. In 2002, God called me out of corporate America into full-time ministry, and I now know that all of that pain and corporate training was preparation for this life phase.

I stand amazed that God could take such a poor, broken woman and use her for His glory. I never take my spiritual or physical health for granted and dutifully take care of my spiritual and physical needs. I thank God every day of my life for giving me one more day free from the terrible, oppressive stronghold of gluttony. Today I no longer sell my soul as cheaply as the price of a cookie. Instead, I use all of it to love and worship the risen Lord.

Road Warrior Worship

I usually drive 30,000 miles per year. There is no telling how many miles I fly. My publisher calls me an author doing research. My husband calls me an apostle. My church calls me a missionary and an evangelist. My daddy just calls me a hobo. I confess that I'm a little of all of the above.

When I'm on the road, I want to be completely in tune with the Spirit of God. Otherwise, how can I do my job? I don't know the people I meet, and they don't know me. I have seconds to allow them to recognize the power of God working through me and to help them relax and let the Holy Spirit work. When God sends exactly the right word at the right moment, they and I know it is God because there is no other way I could have known what to say. My risen Lord sends the words and prepares the hearts, but my soul must embrace His Spirit or I'll miss my cues.

Worship is the secret to my soul embracing the Spirit of God. I worship, listening to my Christian music as I roll down the highway. I shout my praises to God as I do my best not to speed in excitement. You will be glad to know that I do resist raising my hands or closing my eyes while driving and worshipping.

I wake up every morning and have my quiet time with God. Belle yips as she races to our prayer chair. She usually wins, and I have to shoo her down. She reluctantly climbs under the chair. I sit in the chair holding my Bible, usually in the woods, and "lift my eyes to the mountains and let my help come from the Lord" (Psalm 121:1). From time to time, while I'm still worshipping, someone walks up and shares a need. Once, a woman approached and asked, "Do you know how to pray?" Oh, do I know how to pray!

I worship every time I stop Halleluiah. I park, let my feet touch the ground, and breathe in the Holy Spirit. I pray for the people who walked there before and will walk there after. I thank God for being there in that moment. I ask God to prepare the way and send people in need. Unless I'm alone, I usually don't break out in song, but I've been told that I don't need to limit myself or God.

If I just think about my journeys, I begin worshipping. I try to stay in that spirit of constant worship, and want to for the rest of my life, but I must admit to the occasional distraction. When I've been distracted too often, I go away in Halleluiah to worship in the splendor of God's holiness. I return to my life refreshed by the touch of God's wondrous Spirit.

I Have a Complaint

My husband's life scripture is James 1:5–6. We call it the "wisdom scripture," and he applies it to everything. He sums it up in one sentence: "Trust God and don't blink." My complaint is that because he is so committed to not blinking, I have trouble winning an argument, even if I'm right.

Imagine arguing with a man who asks God for wisdom about everything and believes to his toenails that if he allows one single solitary moment of doubt, all will be lost and he will sink into a sea of whirling, twirling waves. I keep explaining that I'm his other half and that if something were so important, God would deliver the wisdom to us both, but if Bob gets the wisdom first, it is almost impossible to get him to see any other side. Occasionally, I'd like him to blink.

The truth of the matter is that while his wisdom does occasionally cross into stubbornness, Bob is the wisest person I know. I watched him go from an insecure, timid young man to having the wisdom of the aged in a matter of days after he discovered that scripture. In his twenties, a woman in our church asked the question, "How can one so young be so wise." Bob and I knew the answer.

Years later, I talked to the corporate executive in charge of the company Bob was working for when he discovered that life-changing scripture. This man said, "I remember Bob when he first started working for us. I didn't think much about him. All of a sudden, things changed, and he became a powerful force to be reckoned with." That statement offered me the opportunity to give testimony to that scripture.

Bob's understanding of James 1:5–6 has matured over the years. He's had to learn the hard way that wisdom not based on knowledge and understanding is probably not God's voice. Battles with humility finally forced him to admit that God occasionally sends His wisdom through the words of others and not directly through Bob's gifted mind. Bob is naturally confident about his own ideas, and one of the hardest lessons for him to learn was that sometimes God sends wisdom to a team and that if his team members disagree with him, Bob might not have the whole story. Bob is good at learning lessons, and I've enjoyed watching his growth. Since Bob's job is to build cars that drive themselves, you should probably be grateful that godly wisdom is important to him.

Progress to—Soul Soothers

POINTS TO PONDER

If you have gotten this far, you are starting to suspect that the secret to every craving, longing, or desire is to turn the focus from trying to satisfy that want or need and to spend that same energy on loving God with every aspect of your makeup—mind, heart, soul, and strength. Loving God with all your soul is the pivotal point in that process. The saying, "Separate the wheat from the chaff," alludes to the ancient process of winnowing the grain to remove the worthless outer covering, the chaff, from the valuable grain.[6] When you love God with all your soul, you separate the wheat from the chaff of your soul. This separation liberates your soul to worship the risen Lord in the splendor of His Holiness and fills every remaining crack and crevice of your heart and mind. The wisdom of God rings loud and clear through the whispering, still small voice of the Holy Spirit.

Step 4

Progress to— Strength Solutions

And thou shalt love the Lord thy God with all thy strength.

—Mark 12:30

Mind ➜ Heart ➜ Soul ➜ Strength

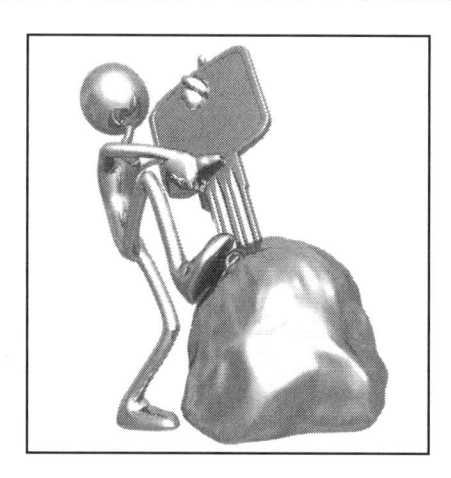

WHEN I COMMITTED to loving God with my mind, heart, and soul, I had more energy than ever before.

The Secret to Everything

Throughout my grandfather's funeral, I'd find myself weeping one moment and directing traffic the next, but my energy was consistently unstoppable. I felt like superwoman during the most difficult moment of my life up to that point. When I asked God for knowledge of His will and the power to carry it out, He granted that request. I not only knew what to do, but also I had power to do things I never thought were possible.

With my newfound strength, I felt like I could move mountains. After the funeral, I began the process of applying that lesson to the rest of my life. First, I tackled my marriage. I'd resented the fact that while I lay sick in bed Bob's career had soared. I was furious about the number of hours Bob worked. I didn't want to be angry at Bob anymore, so we got counseling. It turned out that my anger had caused most of the problems, and when I got over it, Bob wanted to spend time with me. Wonder of wonders, in 1984, we started a business together. And would you believe that he actually ended up reporting to me? We worked side by side for the next seventeen years, working tirelessly and growing a successful software business. This poor woman, formerly bedridden, was wearing suits and wheeling and dealing in the corporate world. The best part was that like my grandparents, my husband and I loved working and playing together.

Now, I travel the country as a missionary, speaker, and author. People who travel with me are astounded at how hard and tiring it is, but God grants the energy to do what I need to do. People call me bold, and I just laugh and tell them that the Holy Spirit is bold. I just try to stay out of the way. People say I have high energy, but I remind them that the strength of Christ is unlimited. I know that by myself, I was sick and lying in bed with people taking care of me.

Progress to—Strength Solutions

Are you tired? Look around. People are exhausted. Both marriage partners work. Children do homework in cars on the way to soccer practices. Women trudge up corporate ladders while homes, children, husbands, and communities tug on their apron strings. Husbands change diapers while balancing computers on their laps. "Having it all" morphs into "doing it all," and America's shoulders stoop from trying to meet the demands of their days.

The other side of the driving, overachieving lifestyle is to stop trying altogether. Words like "I'm not going to be trapped by society's demands" become excuses for wasting precious time that God gave us to live and work on earth. The spectrum between those two extremes is wider than from the heavens to the earth, but the same thing—response to earthly demands on time—drives both extremes.

> ### The Secret To Living In a Busy Society
> **Love God with all your strength, and let God's strength replace yours.**

So what is the secret to living in such a busy society? Surely it cannot be to quit your jobs, neglect your families, or sacrifice everything to join the other proverbial rats racing each other for success. The secret is to love God with all your strength and let God's strength replace yours.

> **God will give you the courage to take the risks you need to succeed.**

The Secret to Everything

In Step 4, you serve God by allowing His strength to replace your strength. The promise of Step 4 is that God will give you the courage to take the risks you need to succeed. The purpose is to harness the power of God to fulfill your missions in the world.

Look at the now famous hardworking disciples. After the disciples met the risen Lord and began loving God with their entire minds, hearts, and souls, they became unstoppable. The risen Lord sent the Holy Spirit, who began empowering them minute by minute, step by step. They walked from city to city, proclaiming the name of Jesus. Their courage was astounding in the face of threats of prison, torture, and death. They worked tirelessly everywhere they went. Where did that strength and courage come from? It came from the risen Lord.

If you've embraced Step 1, you've discovered that you can love God with your entire mind by focusing your mind on God's will. In Step 2, you experienced the beginnings of emotional balance as you let go of past hurts and resentments and began loving God with all your heart. In Step 3, you eliminated strongholds and time wasters as you began to know the essence of your soul and love the risen Lord with all your soul. In short, when you know what to do, doing it is easy. All you have to do is allow God to supply you with the strength to do it.

When you love God with your entire mind, heart, soul, and strength, your strength will become like Jesus feeding five thousand people with a few tiny fish and loaves. Jesus blesses it, and there is enough to go around. Energy replaces exhaustion as your mind, heart, spirit, and body grow stronger and more useful. You will dance your way through your days with a power and strength beyond your wildest imagination. You will serve God, letting His strength replace your strength.

Progress to—Strength Solutions

Primary Principle: God Provides the Strength

Memory Verse:

> If anyone serves, he should do it with the strength God provides, so that in all things God may be praised through Jesus Christ. To him be the glory and the power for ever and ever.
>
> —1 Peter 4:11

If you have been faithfully reading this book, you may be getting a glimpse of what God has in store for you. At this point, you may be screaming, "But wait. I'm too weak. I'll never make it." If you think you are too weak to change, I couldn't agree more. You will not hear any of the popular self-help platitudes about what *we* can accomplish from me. As you read in Step 3, *my own* strength landed me in bed with my mother raising my children. God's strength propelled me into becoming the mother, wife, church member, business woman, and minister God intended, and He enabled me to hike mountains (albeit, small ones).

However, there is a Bible promise you can depend on. Through the strength of Christ, you *can* do all things (Philippians 4:13). That confidence is yours through Christ before God (2 Corinthians 3:4). The best part is that when you serve the world with the strength God provides, God is praised through Jesus Christ (1 Peter 4:11). You win and God wins.

So are you feeling like a super hero yet? You should be. Read your Bible. The strength of God moves mountains, parts seas, and allows you to walk on water. Could there be a better secret weapon? You can have the confidence to know you can do all things; and when you move those mountains and part those seas, you have the privilege of your actions praising God and not you. Toss off that life jacket of fear and proceed in faith to walking on water.

The Secret to Everything

Purpose: Ministry

Discipleship → Fellowship → Worship → Ministry

> Each one should use whatever gift he has received to serve others, faithfully administering God's grace in its various forms
>
> —1 Peter 4:10–11

True ministry is service to others. Ministry is the common, everyday duties you perform to fulfill your part in society. God gives you gifts so you can serve others. The purposes of the first three points, discipleship, fellowship, and worship, are to prepare you for ministry. You followed Christ, and as your fellowship with Him deepened, you began worshipping the risen Lord. True ministry that relies solely on God begins after you have met the risen Lord in Step 3.

I found out the hard way to beware of counterfeit ministry. While true ministry is service, not all service is ministry. There was a time in my life when my service to others left me exhausted and resentful. Service to others that depended on my own strength wore me out while never allowing me to stop. Words like "codependent" floated through my head. A codependent person is psychologically dependent in an unhealthy way on meeting the needs of someone who is addicted or practicing unhealthy behaviors.[7] My actions seemed godly, but my motives for service were not.

At one time, I needed the praise of others to build my own poor self-esteem. In a desperate effort to win friendship, I even offered to give a baby shower for a woman I'd just met. I'll never forget the humiliation I felt when I saw the surprised expression on her face. I knew she saw through my motives and felt sorry for me. The need for this kind of affirmation flashed like a neon sign advertising my shameful need for affirmation. My deeds often looked good, but in truth, they enabled people to depend on me instead of God. When I realized that I could potentially have the mind of Christ and do all things through Christ, the need for the praise of the world began to melt away. Affirmations were a poor substitute for the joy of loving God with my entire strength.

Service powered under your own steam is limited to your own energy and motives and often runs out of fuel right in the middle of projects. Self-propulsion leaves college degrees unfinished, church commitments unmet, and children neglected. While actions begin with good intentions and some get farther than others, the results usually fall far short of the goals.

When you discover the strength provided by the risen Lord, your perspective changes and actions become about ministering to others rather than about improving your personal situation. When your purpose is godly ministry, frustrations and pains lose their power to trip you as they become stepping-stones for meeting the needs of others.

> **The Secret Key to True Ministry: Love God with all your strength**

Ministry is taking your place in the world and doing your part to meet the needs of others. Where codependent people become doormats for all to walk on, ministers soar on eagle's wings, running and not growing weary (Isaiah 40:31). For ministers, their professional, church, and family lives all become part of their ministry callings. When you spend every minute of every day with ministry as your purpose, ordinary tasks and even annoying experiences become joyful opportunities for service. Ministry can be as simple as vacuuming the house or as sophisticated as running a homeless shelter. Ministry includes your job, callings, and the roles you play in the lives of others. The secret key to true ministry is to love God with all your strength.

Promise: Courage

Knowledge → Understanding → Wisdom → Courage

Memory Verse:

> Have I not commanded you? Be strong and courageous. Do not be terrified; do not be discouraged, for the Lord your God will be with you wherever you go.
>
> —Joshua 1:9

When you gain knowledge, understanding, and wisdom, you will know what to do next. If you go no further, never putting feet to the wisdom of God, knowledge, understanding, and wisdom become bitter pills that feed guilt, poor self-esteem, and hopelessness. In fact, suffering from poor self-esteem provides clues for what you should be working on in relationship to your walk with God.

Taking the next steps and obeying God can be terrifying. The secret to forward progress is courage, and the secret to courage is action. Since God combined strength with courage thirty-six times in the Bible, you can see why it is important to understand the connection between courage and strength. Courage is the result of loving God with your entire strength; but letting fear stop you tosses you back onto the tottering seesaw of spiritual, emotional, mental, and physical imbalance. Paradoxically,

Progress to—Strength Solutions

courage is the promise of Step 4, but you usually get it *after* you serve God, letting His strength replace yours.

While travelling the country as a missionary, often my *adventures* become more *exciting* than I or others are comfortable with. The world is dangerous, and if I dwelled on everything that could happen, I would never leave home. Instead, I try to love God with my strength, do what God says, and when I look back, I realize I acted courageously. An overused saying comes to mind, "Courage is fear that has said its prayers."[8]

People say I am courageous to travel alone. I laugh. Without God, I'm a trembling coward. As a young mother, I was a tangled web of fears, obsessions, strongholds, and inactivity. Many times during my years as a stunted Christian, God and I would have a reckoning. I cried out for help. He answered and gave me knowledge (Step 1) of His will for me. He even gave me understanding (Step 2) for why I should do something and the wisdom (Step 3) to know how. Unfortunately, fears repeatedly brought each good intention to a screeching halt.

For example:

- I was so afraid to stay alone that I begged my husband not to take business trips. *Imagine* me sleeping alone in a tent if I couldn't sleep alone in my own bedroom.
- I was afraid to drive over bridges. *Imagine* me driving thirty thousand miles per year as a missionary and avoiding bridges!
- I was afraid of people being mad at me. *Imagine* me speaking the true Word of God while being afraid of people getting angry.

I was a Christian who lived as if her Lord were still crucified. Fear meant I had to work twenty-four hours a day keeping my loved ones and myself safe. When I finally understood the unlimited power of the risen Lord, I gave my fears to God and said "yes" to ministry. I finally understood that it wasn't God's goal to keep me out of danger; it was His goal to make me dangerous for the cause of Christ. At first, I trembled as I ventured out. As I began to act and saw the rewards of ministry, my courage grew. One day I woke up and people were calling me "courageous."

> **The secret to having the strength of God is to obey the voice of God.**

Yes, this is indeed a paradox. It takes courage to obey the voice of God, but the courage comes after we obey. The secret to having the strength of God is to obey the voice of God. I agree that I am courageous, but I need to be clear about the source of that courage. My strength and courage come from the risen Lord. I am well aware of the risks I take, but it is no longer the goal of my life to get to the end of my life safely. My strongest desire is to serve God. My biggest fear is *not* obeying God.

Process

> So don't lose a minute in building on what you've been given, complementing your basic faith with good character, spiritual understanding, alert discipline, passionate patience, reverent wonder, warm friendliness, and generous love, each dimension fitting into and developing the others
>
> —2 Peter 1:5–7 (The Message)

Alert Discipline ➔ Passionate Patience ➔ Reverent Wonder

I love the way the paraphrased Bible, *The Message,* writes 2 Peter 1:5–7. You don't want to lose a minute in building on what you've been given. Spiritual growth is a process you build on. In Step 1 you read the above scripture from the *New International* translation of the Bible and talked about faith that led to goodness and knowledge. *The Message* calls it "basic faith" that leads to "good character" and finally to "spiritual understanding."

In Steps 2 and 3, you rid yourself of distractions that stand in the way of fulfilling your ministry. Now you are at Step 4, loving God with all your strength. You are ready to unlock the superhuman strength that is yours through Christ.

Alert Discipline

As you approach Step 4, you use a*lert discipline* to discipline yourself to take this next step. You reel in your impulses and rely on the strength of God. Check your answers against the Word of God, check with a spiritual mentor, take a deep breath, and act—no matter how much it frightens you.

Passionate Patience

When you persevere with *passionate patience,* you make progress. You become like the famous Energizer Bunny[9] that "keeps going and going and going" or the Timex[10] watch that "takes a lickin' and keeps on tickin'." The world may seek earthly power, but you know a secret. By loving God with all your strength, you are "Power" full because the steam of the Holy Spirit powers you.

The Secret to Everything

Reverent Wonder

Few things are as exciting, thrilling, or energizing as r*everent wonder.* A couple of nights before I wrote this, I took a worn out Bible and flipped through it. It was my daily Bible from when God first called me to full-time ministry. As I read my notes and where I had underlined scriptures in relationship to my ministry call, I was filled with reverent wonder. God had spoken through the Holy Spirit and then empowered His instructions to unfold. I shuddered to think that doubt almost stopped me.

Reverent wonder comes after you obey, as you are amazed at what our Savior did through us. Your faith grows when you look back and see what happened. Next time, you act more quickly because you hear God's voice more clearly. More faith leads to less doubt. Eventually, people combine words like "courageous" with your name as you find yourself strong and courageous.

Problems: Yes, But…

Perhaps the most "Yes, Buts" of all come from discussions about strength. "Yes, but" is another word for excuse. You heard my story about the quarters. Quarters began my ministry. My nickname is the "Pocket Full of Quarters Lady" because as I travel, I hand out quarters. God taught me a spiritual lesson through sharing quarters, so I use them in ministry. These quarters represent the free grace of God. They are a metaphor for having full spiritual pockets and help people remember a way to get to my website, www.pocketfullofquarters.com. If I had a quarter for every excuse I've heard as I traveled across America, the "Pocket Full of Quarters Lady" would be rich.

Progress to—Strength Solutions

Yes, But My Temple Walls Have Cracks

> Do you not know that your body is a temple of the Holy Spirit, who is in you, whom you have received from God?
>
> —1 Corinthians 6:19

Our body is the temple of God. Our job is temple maintenance. I try not to be envious when I see the variety of temples God assigned. I wonder why some have cathedrals to maintain while my temple feels like an aging country church with peeling paint. Alas, I have accepted the fact that my job is to do the best I can with what God assigned.

Admittedly, temple walls have cracks, and some age better than others. You might be in poor health, over or under weight, and/or out of shape. An injury or medical surprise may have crumbled some walls beyond repair. To love God with your entire strength, you have to do proper maintenance, repair the walls to the best of your ability, and present God with the best your temple can be.

Temple Repair Kit

- Go to a specialist: Use doctors, nutritionists, physical therapists, or gyms.
- Do what they say: Eat right, exercise, get enough sleep, and follow the doctor's orders.
- Accept your temple: Do the best you can with what you have.
- Get help if you can't follow orders: Twelve-Step Programs, counseling, or mentoring.

Yes, But I'm Sick of Pep Talks

> We do not want you to become lazy, but to imitate those who through faith and patience inherit what has been promised.
>
> —Hebrews 6:12

The Secret to Everything

If people give you pep talks, here is a clue—listen. They might be right. People who love you want you to be your best because they understand the trauma and drama that befall those who are *lazy, slovenly, undisciplined, unorganized, couch potatoes,* or *procrastinators*. For your own good, I am going to give you a pep talk:

- Listen to pep talks, and accept responsibility.
- Confess sin to yourself, God, and a trusted friend or spiritual advisor.
- Ask God to remove the sin.
- Make amends.
- Take classes if you need organizational or skills training.
- Do a little every day.
- Turn off the television and electronic games!

Yes, But I Hate People Telling Me What To Do

> Slaves, obey your earthly masters with respect and fear, and with sincerity of heart, just as you would obey Christ. Obey them not only to win their favor when their eye is on you, but like slaves of Christ, doing the will of God from your heart. Serve wholeheartedly, as if you were serving the Lord, not men.
>
> —Ephesians 6:5–8 (NIV)

Bowing to authority is not easy. At one time, I was the Chief Executive Officer (CEO) of a technology company. I had authority over everyone who reported to me. When we sold our company, I had a boss. A man I barely knew had the right to tell me what to do. I did not agree with many of his decisions and struggled with the balance of doing the right thing while offering the biblical deference required of employees. It's often

Progress to—Strength Solutions

said that former CEOs are the least employable people there are because once a CEO has had that kind of authority, he or she spends the rest of his or her life bucking authority. The Bible tells us to respect authority, and even a former CEO like me should be able to learn to be obedient.

Do not let the independent spirit of living in a free country keep you from the humble deference to authority that is necessary to flourish in any organized society. What many call freedom is really rebellion. Freedom is good, and rebellion is bad. Freedom provides choice and rebellion actually takes it away. The Greek word used for "slave" in Ephesians 6:5 is *doulos*.[11] *Doulos* actually means voluntary or involuntary service and applies equally to our modern day employment system. Unlike the Israelites, who at one time were slaves, Americans are free to choose where we work, worship, and live. Like the Israelites, we are to understand who has authority over us and give deference to that authority.

- Read in the Bible about who has authority (God, pastor, husband, parent, boss…)
- Establish who has biblical authority over you, but certainly do not blindly "follow orders" when it takes you into illegal or immoral realms.
- Obey authority with respect, fear, and a sincere heart.
- Obey not only to win their favor when they are watching but as if you are also doing the will of God, who is always watching.
- Serve wholeheartedly.

Yes, But I Don't Have Enough Time or Money

"For I know the plans I have for you," declares the Lord, "Plans to prosper you and not to harm you, plans to give you hope and a future."

—Jeremiah 29:11–12

The Secret to Everything

I occasionally feel that I don't have enough time or money to accomplish my goals, but I have discovered that God always does. God has plans for me, and His plans include hope and a future. He may not give me everything I think I want, but He always funds and allows the time for His plans.

In fact, God's plans even include prosperity. Before we get too excited, let me say that prosperity may not necessarily mean being rich. I suspect that the word "prosperity" here means we will have enough money, time, and other resources to abundantly fulfill God's plans for our lives.

My experience is that I do not have enough money to fund both God's plan and mine and that I fare best when I toss my plans out the window. The trick is to focus on Steps 1–3 and figure out what God's plans are for me and then focus on Step 4 and obey. The secret to curing my money and time management ailments is to focus my energy on knowing and doing God's will.

If you don't have enough time or money:

- Rely on God's knowledge, understanding, and wisdom to discover God's plans.
- Understand that while you may not have enough time and money to fund those plans, God does.
- Face that every minute and dollar belong to God.
- Use the strength of God to manage His assets to fulfill His ministry call.
- Don't waste any money or time on anything that is not aligned with God's plan.

Yes, But I'm in the Wrong Career/Job

And we know that in all things God works for the good of those who love him, who have been called according to his purpose.

—Romans 8:28–29

Progress to—Strength Solutions

Romans 8:28 promises that everything will work out for your good, but only if you love Him and are called according to His purpose. You may or may not enjoy your current job, but if you have a job to do today, you can rest assured it is God's plan for you to do it.

You may not yet know God's plans for the future, but for today, you can excel where God plants you while watching Him sow new fields for you.

- Define your ministry.
- Decide your current career/job is your ministry calling and that you work for God.
- Since God often reveals His will by starts and stops, ask Him to be clear about your next steps.
- Walk through open doors.
- Graciously walk away from closed doors.
- Work with God's strength.
- Watch new doors open.

Yes, But I'm Too Busy For Church Work

> The world is peripheral to the church. The church is Christ's body.
>
> —Ephesians 1:23 (The Message)

You read the above scripture in the last step. The irony about "being too busy for church work" is that since the world is peripheral to the church, you receive the wisdom and courage to conquer the demon "busy" and accomplish everything you need to do when you:

- Immerse yourself in church.
- Recognize church as the earthly kingdom of God.
- Remember the church is Christ's body.

The Secret to Everything

PRACTICAL APPLICATIONS

RoBob

My dear hardworking Bob builds robots for a living, hence our nickname for him, RoBob. You may find this hard to believe, but building robots is his ministry call. It is the way he serves his fellow man, makes his country better, and supports his family. The call on his life is so strong that he took four years out of a financially lucrative professional career to go back to college to get a PhD in Robotics. I must admit to wondering why building robots was better than his other career, building leading edge software systems, but he was insistent. Once RoBob heard God's voice about robots, nothing could stop him.

I watched RoBob go through the process we've discussed thus far. In fact, his model helped formulate some of the processes written in this book. He started reading articles about robotics (training his mind—Step 1). His interest grew, and before long, he was passionate about robots (emotions—Step 2). Visions of robots danced in his head. He could have gone into robots based on his previous training and experience, but to be the best, RoBob knew he needed another degree. Bob believes that as a Christian, he has a responsibility to be the best he can be at anything he does, so he went into training.

When RoBob talked about going back to school at age fifty, people were quick to offer dire warnings about leaving the corporate world in his fifties. Bob serves a risen Lord, who has the power to do anything. Bob had asked for wisdom (Soul—Step 3) and refused to blink about this call on his life. Those warnings didn't cause any fear or insecurity, and when I say no fear, I mean *no* fear. I wish I were that confident about anything.

At first, school was a little harder than when he was in this twenties, but he quickly got in a groove. He worked hard, day and night (Strength—Step 4), always believing he could do all things through Christ. He didn't just graduate, he ended up being a leader with his younger collegiate peers and still stays in touch with them.

Now, he works in a new leading edge field in a difficult economy but still has no fear for his future. He refuses to worry about the economy or his income. He serves his employer with his whole heart, mentors other businesses and technologists about their place in this budding field, and whistles while he works. When he's out in a field riding on a robotic car that is driving itself, he tries to tell me he's working, but I know he is just a little boy playing with cars.

RoBob sees this robot call as fulfilling his earthly role. God gave him a technical mind, and RoBob feels a responsibility to use it. He sees his job as making life easier and safer for people and businesses, thus serving humankind. He cares about the people he meets and is a role model for staying committed to the call of God. If Bob had said "no" to God about robots, he would have spent the rest of his life regretting it.

Some think that to fulfill a ministry call means they have to abandon a career and go into full-time ministry. If building robots could fulfill a ministry call, so could almost every other career. We are all ministers with ministry opportunities lurking around every corner. Start thinking of your career as your call to ministry, and be the best you can be.

I'm Rusty

Do you ever feel rusty? I'm a fan of the movie *The Wizard of Oz*. Whenever I use the word "rusty," I think of the Tin Man, who constantly needed oil. Like the tin man, I rust easily. I used to play the piano, and even have a degree in it, but I don't practice anymore. Believe me when I tell you I'm rusty at playing the piano.

The Secret to Everything

Several months a year, my life is physical. To travel the country as a missionary, I have to lift, crawl, bend, stretch, hike, and occasionally run for my life. I can't afford to be rusty if I want to be good at what God calls me to do. Part of how we love God with all our strength is to keep our bodies in fit, working condition.

Camping alone is hard work. Putting up a tent is a lesson in dexterity and logic that never came naturally. A camper may seem easier, but there are more things to go wrong or put together. Fitting things into slots and turning knobs the right way is not instinctive to me. Sometimes the tiny doors to compartments and holding tanks open easily, and other times they don't. Hoses don't reach receptacles, get stuck when you try to stow them, and get holes and leak disgusting substances. Leveling blocks under tires shoot backwards many feet when I try to drive up on them, and if I am on top of a mountain, I have to climb down the mountain, usually in the dark, to retrieve them. I won't even go into how heavy camper batteries are or how I have to climb to lower the high hood of Halleluiah.

Much of the ministry time is spent in parks because people go to parks and are usually in good enough moods to talk. Parks require being physical, in the form of hiking, climbing, biking, or running. If I'm in a spiritual conversation with someone who decides to turn left and take a harder trail, I have to go with that person. Running into wild animals on a trail has (on occasion) caused me to actually run.

If I want to keep my poor body moving, I can't afford for it to be rusty. I need my oilcan. My oilcan involves daily stretching, strengthening, and aerobics. It involves eating right, getting enough sleep, and following doctor's orders on various issues. My body does not offer the grace that Jesus Christ does and gets more unruly every day. I have to be diligent.

Progress to—Strength Solutions

I do sometimes wonder why God would call me to such a rugged life and not give me the natural body of an athlete, but who am I to question?

So I get up in the morning and huff and puff through my daily exercise routine. I say "no" to junk food and eat balanced meals. By my estimation, I'm so "good" that I deserve to look and feel like an Olympic athlete, but instead, I just look like me—a lumpy bumpy woman who has to work hard just to stay in good enough physical shape to meet the requirements of her Lord. I rust easily, so I carry my oilcan everywhere. I may not have the strength of an Olympian, but I have a responsibility to offer as much strength as I can to the God whom I love.

Work Hard, Don't Whine, and Appreciate What You Have

The biggest complaint I hear on the road is, "I hate my job." People say their employers make them work too hard, under pay them, and don't appreciate them. I always ask a follow up question about hours worked and salary. I see little difference between people working forty and those working seventy hours a week and making minimum wage or high six figures. The complaints sound eerily alike. Surely, that many people aren't overworked, under paid, and unappreciated.

One day, I asked my daddy, who was born in 1924, if he had liked his job. Daddy spent most of his career on a train. He did every job imaginable, usually riding the same route back and forth day after day. At the end of his career, he had worked his way to a Conductor, and as he put it, "I was the boss of the train." He came home dirty and exhausted. He worked all hours of the night, and they called him in without warning any time they pleased. I lost track of the number of holidays Daddy missed, including the occasional Christmas. He was in several major train accidents and has the scars to prove it.

"What do you mean?" he asked in confusion.

"I mean, did you enjoy going to work every day?"

"*Why* would you ask that?" he asked. "It was my job."

"Most people say they don't like their job," I told him. "They think they're overworked, under paid, and unappreciated. Did you ever feel that way?"

Daddy was speechless. Finally, he said, "I never thought about it. I just went to work and did my job. They paid me good money. They didn't have to appreciate me as long as they paid me."

My father has always been a happy, contented, fun person. He didn't dread his job. Even when he had to miss Christmas day, he was clear that we should be grateful he had a job. I'm not sure I ever heard Daddy whine about his job. I suspect Daddy knows an important secret to loving God with all his strength: work hard, don't whine, and appreciate what you have.

POINTS TO PONDER

God gives more physical strength to some than He does to others. Throughout the course of any life, physical strength ebbs and flows as people age, are injured, have medical problems, and heal. While traveling, I meet many people who are pouting because they do not have the strength of their former years. Once they give in to the pout, self-pity takes over and zaps the rest of their strength, rendering them useless for God and the world.

Another secret to loving God with all your strengths is to use the strength God gives you at any point in time to fulfill His ministry call on your life. Your job is to stay in the best physical condition possible for your particular body. God's job is to power His current ministry call on your life, which He always does.

Step 5

Progress to— Neighbor Needs

Thou shalt love thy neighbor as thyself

—Mark 12:31 (KJV)

MIND ➔ HEART ➔ SOUL ➔ STRENGTH ➔ NEIGHBOR

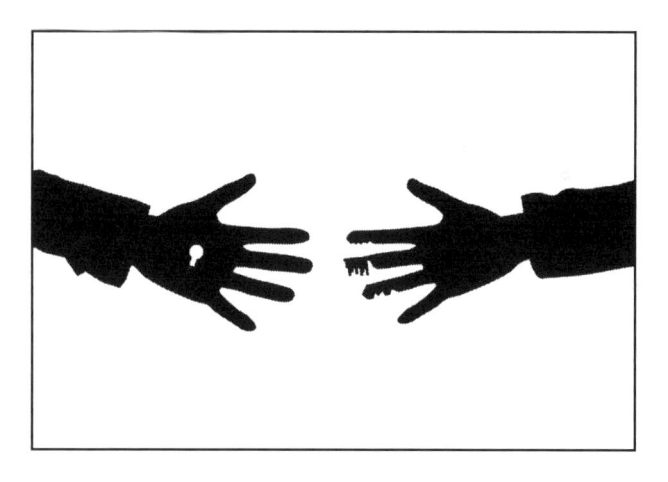

OUR NEIGHBORS ARE a treasure chest waiting to be opened. Being able to love our neighbors as ourselves is the result of working the other four steps. It happens automatically when we love God with all that we are, and when it does, we have truly discovered the secret to everything.

When I stopped working on anything else but loving God, love for my neighbors bubbled over like a steaming pot of boiling water. It happened without any effort. Loving our neighbors as ourselves is the secret treasure that enables us to step outside ourselves and be free to soar like a mighty eagle. Before my experience in the ICU, I wanted everything I didn't have. I wanted a bigger home, a better husband, more children, and a better life. When I got what I wanted, I wanted more, so I was still unhappy. I discovered that what drove me into the hell of gluttony and ill health was that insatiable need for more, more, more. When I found the serenity to accept what I couldn't change and found the courage to change what I could, contentment replaced dissatisfaction and I had the energy to care about people around me. When I cared about the people around me, I started living for possibly the first time in my life.

> ## The Secret
>
> 1. **Stop trying to solve all problems.**
> 2. **Focus all energy on loving God and people more.**

The amazing part of my journey is that by giving up on everything I wanted and surrendering to simply loving God more, I got everything I wanted. Those things I didn't get, I found I no longer wanted. The secret to everything in my life was to stop trying to solve my problems and refocus all my energy on loving God and people more. That is still true today.

When I love my neighbors as myself, I am free from everything that stands in my way. If I serve customers because I

Progress to—Neighbor Needs

love them, meeting their constant demands becomes a joy. If I love my adult children as myself, I stop putting any pressure on them to love me back, and they want to love me back. When I began thinking of my husband as a neighbor, he began to be quite neighborly in return.

Now, God has called me to the streets of America. My last name, Touchton, says it all. I get to touch tons of people. I never forget what it was like to feel so powerless and to be an energy drain to all who love me. My ministry is Pocket Full of Change. We say we change the world one person at a time. I often only have a moment with people, and I want them to make one tiny change toward God. I know it is possible because of what He has done in my own life. Even the most mature and disciplined follower of Christ can always grow closer to being like Jesus. I care about them in a supernatural way that can only come from God, and they sense that love. They know that love could not possibly come from my strength alone. I freely tell my story because I want people to understand the source of any strength they see. As I open the secret treasure to one person at a time, I thank God that He can use someone who had become so useless.

A more challenging question might be, do you love your neighbors enough to let your child die for them? The Primary Principle of Step 5 is that Jesus has the authority to tell you to love your neighbors as yourself. The Purpose of this step is to propel you into the world to fulfill the mission of telling others about Christ. The Promise of this step is that it is possible to experience the continual presence of Jesus in our lives.

When my son Christopher was a senior in high school, he was Captain of his basketball team. He felt a responsibility towards the team and spent much of his time mentoring and tutoring those who needed it. One night, on a bus returning to the school after a game, an altercation broke out between two players. When they arrived at the school, an angry boy rushed to his nearby home instead of going into the locker room to change.

Christopher went inside, dressed, and he and a friend were the first to step out. To his shock, there was his fellow team member, with a gun, waiting to shoot the boy with whom he'd had words. Christopher's companion wanted to leave without getting involved, but Christopher could not leave knowing a shooting was about to take place. In the course of Christopher's trying to talk the boy into giving him the gun, the boy fired the gun. Fortunately, the gunshot warned everyone in the locker room, so the rest of the team stayed inside. The coach joined them outside and talked the young man into giving him the gun.

I was horrified that my son had been that close to a gun being fired. I wanted to pull him out of school and homeschool him, but Christopher would have none of it.

"*Mom*," he said. "I just did what I had to do."

Later, the mother of Christopher's companion and I discussed the incident. She was livid that they had not immediately gotten in their cars and left instead of getting involved. As she said the words, I realized that I wanted my son to love his neighbor as himself, and even if he had been killed, I'd still believe he did the right thing to try to save a life. I said a prayer and left him in school.

Many of us might think we love our neighbors as ourselves, but a more challenging question might be, do we love our neighbors enough to let our children die for them? There may be people we would willingly die for, but giving up our children for someone else, *that* is another story. Isn't that exactly what God did for us when He sent His Son to die on the cross? He offered the death of his Son as a demonstration of His love for us. Most of us have a ways to go before we love anyone that much.

The disciples began their walk with Jesus by brashly proclaiming that they would follow Him anywhere. When the world crucified Him on a bloody hill, their doubt and fear drove

Progress to—Neighbor Needs

them scurrying behind locked doors. The disciple Peter even denied knowing Him. When Jesus emerged from the tomb, the disciples transformed into strong and courageous men on a mission. What changed was that they encountered the risen Lord and suddenly loved their neighbors so much that they had to share their secrets.

If you have moved toward loving God with your entire mind, heart, soul, and strength, love for your neighbors is bubbling up without any effort. Compassion and grace is replacing judgment of others. Mercy is replacing blame. Courage is enabling you to act. An awe-inspiring need to share God's love with the world has awakened your senses to the people and needs around you. You may hear yourself using words like "evangelism," "witnessing," and "plan of salvation."

There are many evangelism classes available. The irony is that if you love God completely, you don't really need them, and if you don't love God more than everything else, they probably won't help. If you have no desire to share Christ with the world, no amount of disciplining yourself or learning evangelistic techniques will motivate you to risk popularity, jobs, or death to talk about spiritual matters. If that is the case, please back up a few steps and work on loving God more. You might still need to work on things like overcoming pride, fear of humiliation, or fear of being judged—possibly the way you judge others—for interfering with what are considered to be personal matters. When you love God completely, nothing can keep you silent. In fact, if you tried to keep silent, "…the stones would cry out" (Luke 19:40).

The secret of this point is, just like a golf swing, nothing works right if you don't follow through. Once you love God enough to want to share His love, if you don't share it with the world, you become spiritually constipated and lose the joy of your Christianity. You go rolling and tumbling back down the steps of the *Sh'ma* or hurling off course on the spiral we call spiritual growth. That means, if you have come this far, you must take this next step if you want to keep your intimacy with God. It may be trite, but to "keep it," you have to "give it away." By "keep it," I'm not referring to salvation, but I am talking about the joy of your salvation. The heartening news is that even if you tumble backwards, because of grace, you can pick yourself up, dust yourself off, and march back up the spiritual ladder of growth.

Primary Principle: Jesus has the Authority

Memory Verse:

> All authority in heaven and on earth has been given to me.
>
> —Matthew 28:18

Jesus has the authority to tell you what to do and how to do it. Step 4 introduced deference to authority. Step 5 is about accepting the ultimate authority, the authority that God delegated to Jesus. Jesus began his final sermon, The Great Commission, by making a bold statement: "All authority in heaven and on earth has been given to me."

Take a moment and let the power of that statement sink into the marrow of your bones. Again, it begs the question, what part of *all* is not clear? Jesus' authority trumps every other authority in your life. That authority is why you can confidently presume that the world needs Jesus as their Savior. It is why you can and should risk your job, reputation, and even your life to tell the world about Jesus. It is why you *must* put aside selfish wants and desires in order to love your neighbors as much as you love yourself. It is why the ultimate demonstration of love of neighbors is your willingness to risk everything to demonstrate the love of Jesus Christ to the world.

Progress to—Neighbor Needs

Purpose: Mission

Discipleship ➔ Fellowship ➔ Worship ➔ Ministry ➔ Mission

Memory Verse:

> Therefore go and make disciples of all nations, baptizing them in the name of the Father and of the Son and of the Holy Spirit, and teaching them to obey everything I have commanded you.
>
> —Matthew 28:19–20

When you love your neighbors, you are a person on a mission. Your mission is to go into the world and make disciples. You introduce your neighbors to God the Father, Son, and Holy Spirit and teach them to obey everything Jesus commanded. You teach them by your words and actions. You are respectful of everyone, guarding your tongue at all times. You live by the "Golden Rule" (treat others the way you want to be treated—paraphrased from Matthew 7:12) and radiate the love of Christ. You feel a burden for the spiritual health of the people around you.

In Christian circles, this mission is called "evangelism." Over the years, the word "evangelize" has developed a negative connotation, right up there with "proselytize." It has become synonymous with anyone using high pressure and even unethical methods to convert people to any cause. The actual definition of "evangelize" it is to preach the gospel or convert to Christianity.[12] The thesaurus offers the words "to preach." In short, evangelism is the best English word to use for your mission from Christ. Evangelizing—converting people to Christianity—is your mission and the ultimate expression of loving your neighbors as yourself.

The Secret to Everything

Promise: Presence

Knowledge → Understanding → Wisdom → Courage → Presence

Memory Verse:

And surely I am with you always, to the very end of the age.

—Matthew 28:20

Jesus closed out the Great Commission, ironically, just before ascending into heaven, with an astounding statement: "I am with you always, to the very end of the age." While He was physically leaving, He promised His continued presence. Jesus loved speaking in absolutes. Not to be redundant, but what part of *always* isn't clear? Let me repeat: Jesus is *always* with you.

Jesus' continual presence is your assurance that you'll know what to say when presented with evangelistic opportunities. Jesus' continued presence is why you would risk your job and/or your life to convert others to Christianity. That presence starts now and goes with you into eternity. When you fully experience His presence, your continued earthly existence takes second place to your mission, because while you could lose your earthly life, you will never, ever lose the presence of Jesus. In fact, it is only by fulfilling your mission, called the Great Commission, that you fully experience the Presence of Jesus Christ.

Process

For this very reason, make every effort to add to your faith goodness; and to goodness, knowledge; and to knowledge, self-control; and to self-control, perseverance; and to perseverance, godliness; and to godliness, brotherly kindness; and to brotherly kindness, love. For if you possess these qualities in increasing measure, they will keep you from being ineffective and unproductive in your knowledge of our Lord Jesus Christ. But if anyone does not have them, he is nearsighted and blind, and has forgotten that he has been cleansed from his past sins.

—2 Peter 1:5–9

Brotherly Kindness ➔ Love ➔ Knowledge of Jesus Christ

This is the longest section of this book because it is the most exciting. Think about it, you can experience love and intimate knowledge of Jesus Christ. Look at 2 Peter 1:5–9 one more time. Step 1 discussed the first three words in the progression: Faith ➔ Goodness ➔ Knowledge. Knowledge was the promise of loving God with all your mind. In Step 4, loving God with all your strength, we talked about the next three words in the progression. Self-control leads to perseverance, which leads to Godliness.

The final progression is the last three words: Brotherly Kindness ➔ Love ➔ Knowledge of Jesus Christ. What starts as brotherly kindness turns into deep love for your neighbors. When you finally experience that love, you have knowledge of Jesus Christ and want to shout it from the mountaintops. Note the warning at the end of the scripture. If you do not have this level of intimacy with Jesus, you are nearsighted and blind. You have forgotten that God cleansed you from sin and have lost the joy of your salvation. When you have the joy of your salvation, you become an evangelist.

Evangelism

I'm often introduced as an evangelist. The first time I heard it, I gasped. Since I thought of evangelists as amazing people like Billy Graham, that introduction disturbed me. Once I understood the definition, being a conduit for people converting to Christianity, I welcomed the title.

My call to ministry beckons from the streets of America. What keeps me awake at night is communicating to others the beautiful, peaceful, exciting, life-changing, and fulfilling relationship possible with Jesus. Loving Him with my entire mind, heart, soul, and strength has filled every dark corner of my existence and driven me to care so deeply for my neighbors that I would leave my comfortable world behind, take risks with my life, and travel the streets of America.

My call is to Christians and non-Christians because everyone needs to love God more. When I think of "converting people to Christianity," I think not only in terms of converting non-Christians to Christianity but also in terms of converting Christians so they can experience Christianity in the fullest sense possible. If Christians loved God with their entire minds, hearts, souls, and strength, the light of Christ would burn so brightly that it would sear darkness out of every soul.

I've taken many courses on evangelism, and every technique I've ever studied worked as long as I used it. There is no "right" way to evangelize, but there is a "right" message to teach. People often ask what technique I use the most. The answer is that it varies with the situation. Below are some techniques I've come to depend on. Forgive the corny titles.

Cookbook Evangelism

> For God so loved the world, that he gave his only begotten Son, that whosoever believeth in him should not perish, but have everlasting life.
>
> —John 3:16 (KJV)

Cookbook Evangelism is my name for a systematic approach to evangelism. It is what you probably think of when you use the word "evangelism." Evangelical Christians take classes to learn these techniques. A plethora of pamphlets and tracts that fit inside pockets, purses, and briefcases are available to help with the process. Most of these pamphlets begin with an attention-getting question and end with a prayer, inviting Jesus into a life. All of them contain Scripture verses. It is the most common technique taught and used. In recent years, it has been highly criticized, even by evangelical Christians. Because it does not always work or others react negatively to what they call a "canned approach," it has lost favor with many Christians.

Admittedly, it is a simple approach, but beginning a walk with Jesus is simple. This process does still work, and I often use it. Instead of "throwing the baby out with the bath water" and rejecting this approach completely, perhaps it is better to understand when and how to use it.

Converting people to Christianity is a process analogous to gardening. Some plant seeds, water, tend the garden, or harvest. Cookbook evangelism is the "harvesting" of our "conversion garden." I use it when someone appears ripe and ready to invite Jesus into his or her life.

So how do we know when people are ready? That is an easy question. We ask. As of this writing, in all my conversations across all fifty states I've only had one person act offended and tell me to mind my own business. Even that person, after we spent more time together, eventually discussed Christianity.

Below is how I practice Cookbook Evangelism:

1. *Relationship*: I begin a conversation about something we have in common or are enjoying. Conversation starters include nature trails, clothes, children, or sunsets.
2. *Introductions*: I include my identity with Christ as a part of my introduction. For example, "My name is Cheryle Touchton. I'm from Jacksonville, Florida. I'm a Christian, wife, mother, and grandmother."

The Secret to Everything

3. *Question*: I ask, "Are you Christian?"
4. *Listen*: I listen carefully to the answer.
5. *Prayer*: I silently pray for the right words to say.
6. *Question*: I ask, "May I tell you what I meant by the question?"
7. *Action*: Amazingly, most answer an eager "yes."
   a. If the person says "yes," I proceed to the next step.
   b. If the person says "no," I ask if I could give them a pamphlet to read later.
8. *Definition*: I say, "I have a simple definition of Christianity. The Bible says a Christian is someone who:
   a. Believes in the birth, death, and resurrection of Jesus Christ,
   b. Has confessed sin and a need for Jesus in his or her life,
   c. And has asked Jesus to be the Savior and Lord of his or her life."
9. *Ask*: I ask, "By that definition, are you a Christian?"
10. *Listen*: Again, I listen carefully.
11. *Action*: If the answer is "no," I do what sales people would call "calling the question." I ask, "We could do that right now. Are you willing?"
    a. If the person says "yes," I pull out a pamphlet that has scriptures in it and walk the person through the steps to salvation, praying with him or her at the end. I always leave the pamphlet with the person.
    b. If the person says "no," I ask if I can leave him or her with a pamphlet and a way to e-mail me with further questions.

Drive-by Evangelism

A farmer went out to sow his seed. As he was scattering the seed, some fell along the path, and the birds came and ate it up. Some fell on rocky places, where it did not have much

Progress to—Neighbor Needs

soil. It sprang up quickly, because the soil was shallow. But when the sun came up, the plants were scorched, and they withered because they had no root. Other seed fell among thorns, which grew up and choked the plants. Still other seed fell on good soil, where it produced a crop—a hundred, sixty or thirty times what was sown. He who has ears, let him hear.

—Matthew 13:3–9

Drive by evangelism is what I call "seeding the garden." It is easy to speak a quick word about Jesus everywhere we go. I think of it as tossing out seeds. Some seeds fall on fertile soil and others on dry soil. Often that quick word leads to a longer conversation in which I can use another technique.

Examples
- Check Out Clerk: Thank you. I'm a Christian, and I'm going to pray for you as I walk out.
- Wait Staff: I'm a Christian. We're about to say a blessing. Is there anything you need prayer for?
- The Bank: Thank you. I'm a Christian. I'm going to do my best to use this money for God's glory.

Jesus Style Evangelism

Jesus said to her, "You are right when you say you have no husband. The fact is, you have had five husbands, and the man you now have is not your husband. What you have just said is quite true."

—John 4:17–18

When Jesus met a woman at the well, he used an ordinary situation, getting water, to help her find salvation. He boldly confronted and then offered a solution. Jesus used stories and parables to make points about what He noticed in the people with whom He interacted. He usually focused on one aspect of their spiritual lives, but He always addressed the issue that was standing between the individual and God. Jesus was observant and used what He saw. He noticed people in need and offered answers to their struggles. He knew the Scriptures and wove them into the conversation, often without even identifying them as Scripture. The Holy Spirit guided Him in these conversations and will guide us too.

This approach takes time, a comfortable speaking knowledge of the parables and stories of the Bible, a willingness to share personal stories, keen observation skills, and listening to the Holy Spirit. It is my favorite evangelistic style, and while using it, I stay alert for when it is time to change to the simple "Cookbook Evangelism" and offer what I call "The Plan of Salvation."

1. *Ask*: Every morning, I ask God to send opportunities.
2. *Watch*: I watch for:
   a. People in need.
   b. People doing dangerous, hurtful, or annoying things that Christians label as sin.
   c. People with the stooped shoulders of stress, grief, or pain.
3. *Prayer*: I silently pray for the right words to say.
4. *Speak*: People say I'm blunt, but I say I'm bold. I speak what I observe. Examples:
   a. "I can't help seeing the circles under your eyes. You look like something is worrying you."
   b. "You look lost. May I help?"
   c. "You are having trouble carrying those groceries. May I help?"
   d. "I noticed the tattoos. What do they mean?"
   e. "You look like you are in pain. Do you need prayer?"

Progress to—Neighbor Needs

5. *Explain*: When a person looks startled by this personal intrusion, I explain, "I'm Cheryle Touchton. I'm a Christian, so I'm supposed to help where I can. I noticed you, so I had to talk to you."
6. *Holy Spirit Hook*: I make small talk until I feel the Holy Spirit take charge. There is usually a point where the conversation turns serious or emotional. When it does, I listen and point out what I hear and/or observe. Examples:
    a. "Wow. The tears let me know you are still bothered by what happened ten years ago."
    b. "It must be tough to have so much to do. You look exhausted."
    c. "You winced when you said that. It still hurts."
    d. "You looked away when you said that. Do you feel guilty?"
7. *Listen*: At that point, all I have to do is to listen until the person starts, repeating him or herself. A dam bursts, and words often pour out. While the person talks, I listen and pray to know how to respond.
8. *Hope Offering*: Because Jesus is always with me, He supplies the words. Because it is so spontaneous, the person knows the Holy Spirit is working, and we both are in awe. I offer words of hope in the form of:
    a. A personal story from my life.
    b. A personal story of someone I know.
    c. A biblical example of hope.
9. *Next Step*: I leave the person with something to do. Examples:
    a. Church: We talk about how church helps and what the Bible says about church.
    b. Scripture: I offer scriptures. Being prepared is essential. We can prepare by memorizing scriptures.

> I carry tiny scriptural reference cards for some of the more common difficulties people struggle with.
>
> c. Salvation: If applicable, I offer to pray with them to receive Jesus.
> d. Resources: I make suggestions about counseling, Twelve-Step Recovery Programs, or Crisis Hot Lines. I carry tiny resource cards with phone numbers.

Lighthouse Evangelism

> For God, who said, "Let light shine out of darkness," made his light shine in our hearts to give us the light of the knowledge of the glory of God in the face of Christ. But we have this treasure in jars of clay to show that this all-surpassing power is from God and not from us.
>
> —2 Corinthians 4:6–7

A more common name for this is "Life Style" evangelism, and simply put, it means living a Christ-like life that is a witness to the world. I prefer the term "Lighthouse" because I believe we are supposed to be the blinking, blaring light of Christ in the world.

I hear people say, "I do not have the gift of evangelism, but at least I try to live my life in such a way that others will be touched by it." Aggressive evangelicals call that an excuse for not evangelizing, but I think it is a perfectly reasonable way to evangelize *if*:

1. We make sure the name of Christ is associated with us.
2. Our life is above reproach.
3. Love for others radiates from our pores.

If we claim this style of evangelism as our primary approach and do not speak the name of Christ aloud, people will assume

Progress to—Neighbor Needs

we are naturally nice people and give the credit to us instead of God. Going to church is a great witness, but it is not enough. Many nice people go to church. We must work the name of Jesus Christ into our everyday conversation and have Christian literature available to hand out.

Example

When people thank you for helping, laugh and say, "You can thank me if you want, but I'm a Christian, and this is just what we do. If you want to know how to become a Christian, I have a pamphlet in my car."

Jesus-on-the-Spot Evangelism

> On reaching Jerusalem, Jesus entered the temple area and began driving out those who were buying and selling there. He overturned the tables of the money changers and the benches of those selling doves, and would not allow anyone to carry merchandise through the temple courts. And as he taught them, he said, "Is it not written: 'My house will be called a house of prayer for all nations?' But you have made it 'a den of robbers.'"
>
> —Mark 11:15–17

When Jesus entered the temple and saw the corruption, He threw a fit. While quoting Scripture, He overturned tables and tossed coins away. As Christians, there are some things we must refuse or stop. It becomes evangelism when we speak the name of Christ as the reason for our outrage and actions. "Jesus-on-the-Spot Evangelism" is doing what Jesus would do in the same circumstances.

Examples

- When you spot something that is wrong, get angry (but do not sin).

The Secret to Everything

- Take action to stop what is happening.
- Speak the name of Christ and quote Scripture as you take action.

PROBLEMS: YES, BUT...

When we start talking about loving others, "Yes, buts" abound. They get worse if we talk about evangelism.

Yes, But I Didn't Go to Kindergarten

Golden Rule:

> So in everything, do to others what you would have them do to you, for this sums up the Law and the Prophets.
>
> —Matthew 7:12

Being polite and having manners is critical to demonstrating love for our neighbors. It is the demonstration of brotherly kindness. The title of the popular book *All I Really Needed to Know I Learned in Kindergarten* by Robert Fulghum says it all. Perhaps kindergarten lessons are the best practical applications of the Golden Rule. My husband, Bob, says that the fact that his parents never sent him to kindergarten is why he is so evangelically challenged. So, in case you, like Bob, didn't go to kindergarten or read the book, below is a list of kindergarten tips:

- Say "please" and "thank you."
- Wait your turn.
- Don't hit, shove, or spit.
- Say you're sorry when you hurt someone.
- Clean up your own mess.
- Don't take things that don't belong to you.
- Play fair.

Progress to—Neighbor Needs

Yes, But People Keep Calling Me "The Church Lady"

> How can you say to your brother, "Brother, let me take the speck out of your eye," when you yourself fail to see the plank in your own eye? You hypocrite, first take the plank out of your eye, and then you will see clearly to remove the speck from your brother's eye.
>
> —Luke 6:42

The Church Lady was a popular and amusing character from the secular television show *Saturday Night Live*. I'm not a fan of this show, but this character intrigued me. The Church Lady thought she was good but was instead rigid and judgmental, always telling people what they *should* do. She is the secular world's equivalent of the Pharisees who gave Jesus so much trouble. She completely forgot to read Luke 6:42 or she would have understood that before she could criticize anyone, she had be perfect herself. The Bible does not actually tell us not to judge. It tells us not to judge unless we are already perfect and that if we judge, we must be willing for that judgment to fall on us.

The "Church Lady" approach to life does not help anyone. When we pass judgment on others, judgment seeps out of our pores and irritates everyone it touches. It interferes with our ability to influence others. When we truly love our neighbors as ourselves and practice the golden rule (treat others the way we want to be treated), there is no room for judgment. Judgment gets in the way of perfect love.

If you resemble The Church Lady:

- Stop telling people what to do.
- Stop obsessing about what they should do.
- Focus your energy on removing the "plank from your own eye."

The Secret to Everything

Yes, But I Don't/Won't/Can't Evangelize!

Unfortunately, if you don't share your faith with others, you are in the majority. If you've never shared your faith, you may have no idea how easy or rewarding it can be.

Excuse 1: I Don't Have the Spiritual Gift of Evangelism

The Great Commission does not come with the label: Only for those with the gift of evangelism. If you hear yourself saying these words, focus more energy on loving God with your entire mind, heart, soul, and strength. Meditate on the wonder of your faith. Remember:

- Our Savior rose from the dead.
- Jesus commanded everyone to go out into the world.
- He goes with you.
- If you love God with all your mind, heart, soul, and strength, you'll be so intimate with Him that nothing could keep you silent.

Excuse 2: I'll Lose My Job If I Evangelize

The evangelism excuse I hear most frequently is, "I'm not allowed to talk about my faith at work. I could lose my job." The difficult truth is that when you fulfill your mission as a Christian, you might lose your job or something worse, but when you love God with all your mind, heart, soul, and strength, obedience to Christ will become more important than anything.

If job restrictions are keeping you silent about your faith, remember:

- Our Savior died for us.
- All but one disciple died getting the message to you.
- Martyrs and missionaries have died for the cause of Christ for centuries.

- Losing a job is a small price to pay for being obedient and leading someone to Christ.
- Be shrewd (Matthew 10:16). Evangelize with good sense and finesse, and maybe you won't have to lose your job.

Excuse 3: I'll Offend People If I Evangelize

Our world pressures us to be "politically correct." Being politically correct means we word things in such a way as to minimize social offense. An ever-changing list of safe words, opinions, and doctrines circulate and are curriculum for business, college, and church classes. My experience on the streets of America is that when I am respectful of others and demonstrate love, few are offended.

If you are worrying about offending people:

- Ask yourself: would you rather be politically correct or obedient?
- Trust that if you talk about Jesus without judging, people are rarely offended.
- Remind yourself that worrying about offending people is fear and rebuke it!

Excuse 4: I Won't Know What to Say If I Evangelize

Jesus promised to be with you always. He will supply the words. When He does, you will be so amazed at the results that you will let Him do it more often. If you are worried about what to say:

- Trust Jesus to supply the words.
- Pick the evangelistic style that works for the situation.
- Ask the Holy Spirit what to say.
- Open your mouth, and let God do the rest.

The Secret to Everything

PRACTICAL APPLICATIONS

When people travel with me when I am on the road as a missionary, they usually notice two things: Evangelizing is easier than they thought. And traveling is harder. Below are some real life evangelism stories.

Cookbook Evangelism

"If you died today, would you go to heaven?" That was the opening question at the Inside Out Ministries booth on the mall in Washington DC. I first met Inside Out Ministries in Seattle, Washington, and they invited me to join them in Washington DC on July 4th of 2008. I happily drove across the country to be there. They were one of several Christian ministries participating in DC's annual Freedom Fest.

"Why do you believe that?" was their follow-up question. Inside Out team members stood outside the booth, inviting people to take the two-question test. Those who came to the booth eagerly answered the questions to the best of their abilities and then listened to the Bible's answers. Like a recipe in a cookbook, Inside Out Ministries had the plan of salvation carefully typed up in a binder. Each page was printed twice so both the presenter and those presented to could see the same text.

Is the approach too simple? The Bible says by our fruits we shall be known. The fruits of this approach were obvious as person after person listened and prayed to become a Christian. Talk about going into the world to make disciples of all nations—the world comes to Washington DC on July 4, where Christians were eagerly waiting on the mall outside the Capital building to give the good news of Christ.

As I participated and watched, I was overwhelmed by the privilege of getting to be a part of something so powerful. After

Progress to—Neighbor Needs

several had prayed to receive Jesus, I turned to an Inside Out team member and said, "This is amazing."

She agreed. "It's like this every year. God sends the people who are ready to our booth."

It was true. Many who came to the booth were ready to hear about Jesus and to ask Him to be a part of their lives. Each had his or her story about how God had prepared them.

A Hindu man from India walked up to the booth, and I invited him to take the test. Then I said, "If you died today, would you go to heaven?"

"I don't know," he said. "That's why I'm here." At the same event the previous year, someone had given him a Bible. "I tried to read it," he said. "I couldn't understand it."

"That's because you were trying to read it alone. You didn't have the help of the Holy Spirit or other Christians. Would you like me to help you?" I asked.

He nodded eagerly.

I walked him through some scriptures. I told him about Jesus dying for his sins and that when you accept Jesus, you receive the Holy Spirit. I explained that I was there because the love of Jesus was inside me. I used the words Inside Out Ministries supplied to walk him through the scriptures that explained all have sinned and that he needed to confess his sins, repent, believe in Jesus, and invite Jesus into his life.

"Salvation is free," I said. "It is simple. You don't have to work for it. All you have to do is ask. Would you like to become a Christian right now?"

"I would," he said.

Slowly I read the printed prayer, and he solemnly repeated the words after me. We spent a few minutes talking about finding a church, baptism, Bible study, and daily time with God. He went away smiling.

At other booths, other Christians were experiencing the same thing. They had pamphlets in other languages and a

The Secret to Everything

Spanish-speaking booth. I left that day with my heart full and overflowing, thanking God for letting me witness and participate with these faithful Christians in action.

Drive-by Evangelism

I was sitting with Christian friends in a restaurant, and the waiter walked up. I said, "We are Christians. We're about to say a blessing. Is there anything we can pray for you?"

"No," he said while quickly backing up.

"*That went well,*" I joked sardonically to my friends. We said our blessing and began eating.

A few minutes later, the waiter came back. "I didn't give you a very good answer," he said. "I need a lot of prayer. I'm in school and don't know what to do with my life. I have a friend who is sick, and I'm worried about him."

"We'll pray for you right now," I offered. He had to go back to work, so I left a Christian tract on the table.

Jesus Style Evangelism

Belle and I frolicked by Lake Ontario in New York as we watched the sunset sprinkle diamond-faceted rays across the choppy water. While I blew bubbles and Belle chased them, the owner of our campground drove up with her beautiful 8-year-old daughter. The child was wearing a lime green leotard and tights. When she spotted the bubbles and the dog, she ran towards us, and the mother followed. As Belle and the child played, the mother and I talked.

The mother was exhausted. The demands of the campground were getting to her. Money was tight, and time was tighter. She'd grown up in church and was a Christian, but because of running the campground, they were too busy to go to church.

"With my daughter's school, piano lessons, and dance, we just don't have any more time," she explained.

Progress to—Neighbor Needs

"Has your daughter become a Christian?" I asked.

"No," she answered. "She's still young."

I felt my heart breaking for that busy Mom who was juggling so many things. I prayed for the right words to say. Finally I said, "I can see how tired you are, but you are finding time for dance and piano."

"Yes," she said. "I don't want the campground to cause her to miss out."

I looked at the mother and prayed I was expressing the tenderness I was feeling. "Your daughter needs Jesus and church more than she needs dance or piano. There is nothing more important you could do for her than take her to church."

I saw the woman pale with the realization that I was right. I started apologizing for being so direct, but she stopped me.

"No," she said. "You're right. Thank you."

Lighthouse Evangelism

I wish you could meet my friend Jimmy Sullivan. Jimmy is like a neon light for Jesus Christ. When Jimmy talks about Jesus, he always uses both names, Jesus Christ. Jimmy talks about Jesus Christ when he's helping, scolding, or worshipping.

Jimmy lives on the bayous of Houma, Louisiana. He and his wife, Janice, have been married for over fifty years. Jimmy is a man's man. He hunts, fishes, and can build and repair anything. When he and Janice visited us in Phoenix, Jimmy talked Bob into climbing the mountain behind our house. Jimmy taped layers of garbage bags around their ankles and pants legs to ward off the cactus and briers and found big sticks for both to carry. I warned them about rattlesnakes, and Janice and I laughed as we watched them climb the mountain in the Phoenix heat.

Jimmy grew up and became a Christian in the Baptist Church. When he met Janice, he had eyes for no one else. Janice was Catholic, and Jimmy was smitten. He began attending the

Catholic Church with Janice, and a few years after they married, he formally converted. He and Janice are Eucharistic ministers in their parish, where they worship faithfully ever Sunday.

We took a vacation with Janice and Jimmy, and while cruising along in the back seat, Jimmy told a little of his life story. "Jesus Christ goes with me everywhere I go," he said. "There is nothing better you can do than know Jesus Christ."

At their 50th anniversary, after entertaining the crowd with an impressive Jitterbug, Jimmy took the mike and told the 100+ crowd that he hoped they knew Jesus Christ.

If someone's language gets too crass, Jimmy will speak and say, "Enough! I belong to Jesus Christ." He speaks about Jesus Christ on hunting and fishing trips and while helping someone repair their home.

Jimmy doesn't carry a Bible or explain the plan of salvation to anyone. He loves his family and makes sure everyone knows it. He's happy and has fun everywhere he goes. He's ethical and demands ethical behavior of those around him. He speaks his mind, giving both affirmations and scolding if someone needs it. He continually gives credit to Jesus Christ. He is the epitome of what Jesus Christ can do in a life, and it would be impossible not to see Jesus Christ when you are around Jimmy.

Jesus-on-the-Spot

I was in Idaho in a mobile phone store when I heard yelling. I looked up to see an elderly man on oxygen using gnarled hands to prop himself up against the counter. It was a race to see what happened first. Would he pass out, explode, or cry?

The young sales clerk yelled, "That's just the way we do it here, and it's your only choice!"

The man yelled back, "But I can't understand the instructions, and my fingers can't punch the keys fast enough to keep up. My wife just died, and I don't know how to do it."

Progress to—Neighbor Needs

"I can't help you," the sales clerk huffed.

I rushed over to the man, rested my arm gently on his shoulder, and said, "Maybe I can help. What are you trying to do?"

The sales clerk glared and said, "*I'm* handling this."

"No you're not," I said, using what I used to call my "Chief Executive Officer" voice. I knew I sounded firm, but I was serious and wanted to sound like it. "I'm a Christian, and my call from God is to help. This man needs help. I'm going to help this man, and *you* are going to help me help him. One day you will be his age and may need the same kind of help."

The young woman slammed a phone down on the counter. "I don't know what he wants to do, but he needs to use the customer service line."

"Please don't make me listen to all that mumbo jumbo," the man begged. "I tried it at home. I can't do it. I can't keep paying these bills. *Help me.*"

"Whatever you want to do, we'll do it together," I offered. "What do you need?"

"I need these bills to stop coming. I can't afford it," he said. "I don't know why the bills keep coming when I already paid for the phone."

"Have you ever paid bills before?" I asked.

"No," he said. "I just made the money. My wife paid everything."

His name was Ira. I explained how cell phones and their bills worked. I looked at the clerk and asked about Ira's plan.

"I can't tell you anything about his plan," she snapped.

I turned to Ira and said, "Ask what plan you have and what the monthly cost is."

Before Ira could repeat the question, she sighed and said, "*What* is your social security number?"

"I don't know," Ira said.

"It's probably in your wallet," I suggested.

117

"It is," Ira beamed, looking hopeful for the first time. "It's been there since 1944." He pulled out a faded plastic wallet insert containing a tattered social security card.

"I can't get it out," Ira said as he struggled with arthritic fingers. "Would you help?"

"I sure will." I took his wallet and saw a military card. "Did you serve in a war?"

"Yes," he said proudly. "Korea."

"My daddy served in Korea. We," I said, looking pointedly at the clerk, "appreciate your serving your country for us." I got out his social security card and squinted to read the faded numbers. The sales clerk typed away and explained the plan. Ira didn't understand, so I explained again.

"What do you want to do?" I asked.

"I want the bills to stop coming," he said. "I already tried to call the number they gave me, but I couldn't figure out what they were saying."

"He was in last month and was confused. It's not our fault he can't follow instructions," the clerk defended.

"Older people have trouble with automated phone lines," I explained. "They can't hear and don't understand the terminology."

"That's right," said Ira. "I can't do it, and the bills keep coming."

The clerk wouldn't help, but she handed us a phone and number. Together, Ira and I tried to cancel his plan, but he was still under contract.

I hung up and looked at the clerk. "We need to cancel this contract. He tried to cancel last month, so we also need to reduce the bill by that amount."

"I can't," she snapped. "He has a contract."

"Yes, you can," I said. I felt the power of Jesus backing me up and silently claimed the scripture that promised I can do all things through Christ. "This man's wife died. He can't afford the phone. It's the right thing to do, and you will do it."

After some discussion with her manager (that thankfully did not require the company to call a meeting of the Board of Directors), they let him out of his contract and reduced his final bill. I carefully pealed faded money out of his torn and worn wallet. After the bill was paid, Ira had only $4 left in his wallet, but he left happy.

I thanked the sales clerk for finally helping. "As I mentioned earlier, you will eventually be his age. As a Christian, I did what I had to. I hope one day you will understand what I meant."

Points to Ponder

Occasionally, people ask to accompany me for part of my missionary journeys. Halleluiah is tiny, but if the person is female or related to me and wants to participate in the mission, I welcome the company. I do have rules. We do devotions and Bible Study together every morning. We travel listening to Christian music. We worship and pray every time we stop the car and our feet hit the pavement. We ask God to send people in need, and we stay alert so that we can spot them. I warn potential sojourners that I write my adventures until way into the night. The response at the end of the journey is always the same. Traveling, especially the pace I keep, is much harder than they anticipated, and evangelism is easier than they ever suspected.

There is no experience more rewarding than being with someone when the Holy Spirit decides to work in his or her life. True knowledge of Jesus becomes a living Presence in our lives when we pass it to others.

Perseverance: The Next Step

> Consider it pure joy, my brothers, whenever you face trials of many kinds, because you know that the testing of your faith develops perseverance. Perseverance must finish its work so that you may be mature and complete, not lacking anything.
>
> —James 1:2–4

BY NOW, YOU probably have realized the importance of the *Sh'ma* and are starting to understand why Jesus called it The Greatest Commandment. You have learned about those five important words—mind, heart, soul, strength, and neighbor—and what they can mean for you. Now, it is time to continue incorporating the most important commandment into your life, one day at a time.

So how do you persevere in the face of so many distractions and disappointments? For simplicity's sake, we studied a linear stepwise model for living the *Sh'ma* in our everyday lives. This linear model started with loving God with your mind, moved upward to loving Him with your heart, soul, and finally to strength. When you got that far, you found love for your neighbor happened without any effort. Forward progress can be running, dancing, or even trudging upward as long as you keep climbing.

The Step Model

Like any progression, we can make backward and forward progress. We can climb up and down the steps, skip over them, or fall tumbling down.

One day, my seventy-eight-year-old father and I visited the construction site of a house Bob and I were having built. Daddy and I were walking and talking, and I forgot that danger lurks at construction sites. Suddenly, I pitched waist deep into a muddy hole.

"Give me your hand," Daddy quickly commanded as he reached downward.

"*You* can't pull me out," I challenged, futilely trying to pull myself up the slippery side of the hole.

"Give me your hand," he repeated firmly. I looked upward into Daddy's confident, loving eyes and found all the reassurance I needed. I grasped the hand I held as a child, and in a second, I was flying through the air and landing on my feet on safe, secure ground.

"Wow," I explained with the wonder that had worshipped Daddy as a child. "I felt like I was flying. How did you do that?"

"It's all in the leverage," Daddy laughed, never chiding me for briefly losing faith in him. "Are you OK? You're lucky you didn't break your ankle."

Like me plunging into that hole, you may find yourself tumbling back down the ladder of spiritual growth, but God is always reaching out His strong, loving hands to yank you into the safety of His embrace.

Perhaps a Spiral Model would be an even better illustration of applying the *Sh'ma* to the rest of your life.

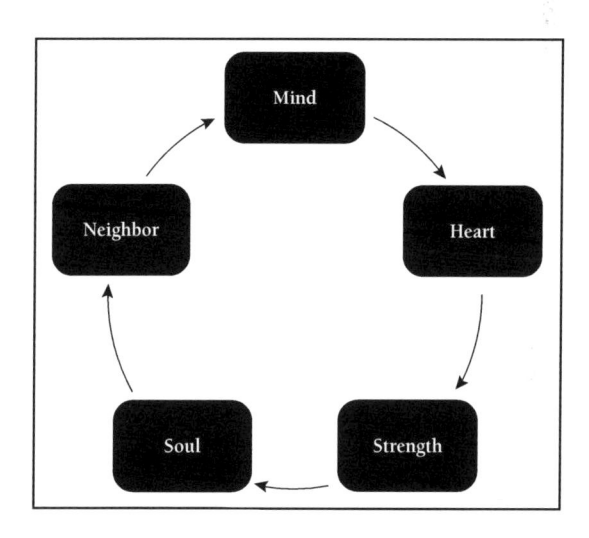

THE SPIRAL MODEL

As you discover what it means to love God with all your mind, heart, soul, and strength, you go round and round, drawing closer and closer to the heart of God. You come face to face with God with your mind. You move forward through the process of loving God with your mind, heart, soul, and strength and finally progress to loving and reaching out to your neighbors.

The Secret to Everything

When you see the power of God working, you are inspired to go deeper into your spiritual journey. You study the Bible to further expand your knowledge. Your emotional heart stabilizes as you begin to understand life events in the perspective of an eternal plan. Compassion for others deepens. Your soul soars with intimate worship that lasts for an eternity. Your strength becomes unstoppable. The depth of your neighborly love astounds you and propels you to go further still. There is no limit to your capacity for love.

As you go around the spiral, you may feel as if you have been rocketed into a fourth dimension or like you are chugging and plugging along. The point of the step and spiral model is to demonstrate how you make forward progress in your spiritual walk with God. From now on, no matter what happens to you, you are going to think first about loving God more instead of solving the problem, handling the difficulty, or jumping the hurdle with your own strength.

St. Augustine of Hippo said, "Love God, and do what you like." The secret formula for *everything* in life is to stop working on *every* problem, issue, challenge, annoyance, disappointment, hurdle, or frustration and start using all your energy to love God more. If you love God with your *entire* mind, heart, soul, and strength, you will automatically love your neighbors as yourself. The secret to applying the secret formula to your life is perseverance, repeating the same pattern one day at a time in every aspect of your life. "Perseverance must finish its work so that we can be mature and complete and not lacking anything" (James 1:4).

PROMISE: ONE MORE TIME

No eye has seen, no ear has heard, no mind has conceived what God has prepared for those who love him.

—1 Corinthians 2:9

Perseverance: The Next Step

There is more to learn, and this is only the beginning of the wonders God has in store for you if you continue on this journey of loving Him more. This ancient, secret formula is changing everything for you, and you have only just begun discovering what it means. From this moment forward, no matter what happens to you, I pray your first response will be about how each experience will help you love God and others more.

Parley

For Group Discussions or Use With a Personal Mentor

Pardon the "Parley." "Discussion" would have been a better title, but I needed one last "P." As a group study, this format provides six one-hour discussion-based group sessions that can be used over a five-week period. The purpose of the group session is spiritual growth and accountability. If no small group is available, use the questions and exercises with a personal mentor.

Group Guidelines

- Keep individual sharing to under three minutes per turn.
- Only share again after everyone has shared.
- Be honest.
- Keep what is said in the group confidential.
- The leader should encourage everyone to share.
- Talk about personal experiences.
- Avoid advice giving or gossip.

The Secret to Everything

Group Format

Session 1

- Open with prayer.
- Promise:
  - What would your life be like if you stopped working on anything else but loving God and people more?

    _____

    _____

  - Read Luke 10:27
  - What is getting in the way of loving God with all your:
    - Mind?

      _____

    - Heart?

      _____

    - Soul?

      _____

    - Strength?

      _____

  - How could you love your neighbors more?

    _____

    _____

Parley

- Preparation
  - Bible Study: Familiarize participants with the P's (Premise, Purpose, Principal, Promise, Process, Problems, Personal Applications) of the five Steps.
  - Remind the group about the memory verses.
- Parley
  - Review group guidelines.
  - Assign homework: read Preparation and Promise and work Step 1.
- Take prayer requests, and pray for specific needs.

Sessions 2–5

- Open with prayer.
- Discussion: Use the discussion questions below.
- Assign Homework: Next Step.
- Take prayer requests, and pray for specific needs.

WEEKLY DISCUSSION QUESTIONS

Progress to Step 1: Mind Matters

1. What does it mean to unlock your mind, and how do you do it?

   _____

   _____

2. Read 1 Corinthians 2:16. What is the mind of Christ like, and how can you have it?

   _____

   _____

The Secret to Everything

3. Read Ephesians 4:22–24. Why is this hard when it looks so simple?
   _____
   _____

4. Read Philippians 4:8. How can we discipline our thoughts to focus on the positive?
   _____
   _____

5. What is distracting your thoughts away from loving God with all your mind?
   _____
   _____

6. List and date your commitments and goals for this step.
   _____
   _____
   _____
   _____

Progress to Step 2: Heart Helps

1. What does it mean to unlock your heart, and how do you it?
   _____
   _____

2. What blocks you from unlocking your heart?
   _____
   _____

3. Read Zephaniah 3:17–18. What do these verses mean for you?
   _____
   _____

Parley

4. Read Galatians 5:22–23. Are your fruits blooming? What would help them produce better?
   _____
   _____

5. Read Ecclesiastes 3:2–8. What did you learn about seasons that you want to share with the group?
   _____
   _____

6. List and date your commitments and goals for this step.
   _____
   _____
   _____
   _____

Progress to Step 3: Soul Soothers

1. What does it mean to unlock your soul, and how do you do it?
   _____
   _____

2. Read Mark 16:6. What is the difference between serving a crucified and a risen Lord?
   _____
   _____

3. Read James 1:5–6.
   a. Do you believe God will supply wisdom?
      _____
      _____

The Secret to Everything

    b. When have you felt like "waves being tossed about in the wind"?
_____
_____

4. What strongholds come between God and you? How do they hurt you?
_____
_____

5. Read Romans 12:6–8. What are your primary spiritual gifts, and how can you use them better?
_____
_____

6. List and date your commitments and goals for this step.
_____
_____
_____
_____

Progress to Step 4: Strength Solutions

1. What does it mean to unlock your strength, and how do you do it?
_____
_____

2. What is draining your energy?
_____
_____

3. What "temple repairs" do you need to make?
_____
_____

4. Read 1 Peter 4:11. What is the difference between serving God using our own strength and serving God using His strength?

5. Read 1 Peter 4:10. How can everything we do be integrated into our ministries?

6. Read 2 Peter 1:5–7 from The Message (written in Step 4). How do you relate to the progression: Alert Discipline→Passionate Patience→Reverent Wonder?

7. List and date your commitments and goals for this step.

Progress to Step 5: Neighbor Needs

1. Why is loving your neighbor the secret treasure?

2. How might you be thinking more about yourself than your neighbor?

The Secret to Everything

3. How can you better love God's children neighbor by neighbor?

4. Read Matthew 28:18–20.
   a. How does believing that Jesus has the authority to send us into the world change our attitude about speaking the name of Christ aloud?

   b. What does loving our neighbors have to do with our mission?

   c. Why does the fact that Jesus is always with us help with our mission to our neighbors?

5. Discuss the various evangelistic techniques from this step.
   a. Which do you practice the most?

   b. What excuses have you been giving for not evangelizing?

   c. What other techniques have you found useful?

Parley

6. List and date your commitments and goals for this step.
   _____
   _____
   _____

7. End with reading the closing—Perseverance: The Next Step. Where are you on the spiral?
   _____
   _____

Endnotes

1. Lan, Ray Vandar, *That the Word May Know—Faith Lesson Video Series*, That the World May Know Ministries, www.followtherabbi.com
2. Traditional US Southern Lullaby, Public Domain, Composer Unknown
3. Niebuhr Reinhold, *The AA Grapevine*, January 1950, 6–7.
4. Abraham Lincoln, 16th President of the United States, (1809-1865)
5. "The Ballad of Jed Clampet," *The Beverly Hillbillies*, Paul Henning, 1962.
6. Gregory Titelman, *America's Popular Sayings* (New York: Random House, 2004), 294.
7. www.dictionary.com
8. Dorothy Bernard
9. Registered trademark from Energizer
10. Registered Trademark of Timex Corporation
11. *Biblesoft's New Exhaustive Strong's Numbers and Concordance with Expanded Greek-Hebrew Dictionary.* Copyright © 1994, 2003, 2006 Biblesoft, Inc. and International Bible Translators, Inc.
12. www.dictionary.com

The Secret to Everything

Pocket Full of Change Ministries

Cheryle M. Touchton is the Director of Pocket Full of Change Ministries. She is an award-winning author and popular speaker for churches, business groups, and Christian television and radio shows. Formerly the Chief Executive Officer of a successful, award-winning software company, Cheryle holds a Masters in Business Administration. The mission at Pocket Full of Change Ministries is to fulfill the Great Commission by helping people, churches, and organizations embrace the Great Commandment, thus empowering them to fill their spiritual pockets so they are prepared for life and eternity. The greatest desire of those in the ministry is to help people discover the power of the *Sh'ma*, the Greatest Commandment, and fully live it in the ordinary circumstances of their lives. Ministry offerings include:

- Coaching individuals and organizations through the process of discovering and implementing God's will.
- Evangelistic, United States-based mission tours.
- Speaking for retreats, special events, television, and radio.
- Web site, blogs, and social networking ministry.
- Creating ministry publications that support the mission of the ministry.

Contact Cheryle@pocketfullofchange.org, or visit pocketfullofchange.org for more information about how Pocket Full of Change Ministries can serve you.

To order additional copies of this book,
please visit our web site at
www.pocketfullofchange.org/book-store

Made in United States
Orlando, FL
08 December 2025